THE BEGINNER'S GUIDE
TO QUANTUM PSYCHOLOGY •••

BY THE SAME AUTHOR

Trances People live:
Healing Approaches in Quantum Psychology

Quantum Consciousness:
The Guide to Experiencing Quantum Psychology

The Dark Side of the Inner Child:
The Next Step

The Tao of Chaos:
Quantum Consciousness, Volume II

Hearts on Fire:
The Tao of Meditation
The Roots of Quantum Psychology

The Way of the Human, Vol. I:
Developing Multi-Dimensional Awareness

The Way of the Human, Vol. II:
The False Core-False Self

The Way of the Human, Vol. III:
Beyond Quantum Psychology

Intimate Relationships:
Why They Do and Do Not Work

I AM THAT I AM:
A Tribute to Sri Nisargadatta Maharaj

THE BEGINNER'S GUIDE TO QUANTUM PSYCHOLOGY

STEPHEN H. WOLINSKY, PH.D.

©2000
Stephen H. Wolinsky, Ph.D.
101 Grand Avenue #11
Capitola, California 95010
Phone: (831) 464-0564
Fax: (831) 479-8233

Cover Art:
M.C. Escher's The Rind
©2000
Cordon Art BV
Baarn - Holland.
All rights reserved.
Printed in Canada

DEDICATION

To the memory of Sri Nisargadatta Maharaj,
the grandfather of Quantum Psychology.

To the memory of my dear friend
Christian who we lovingly called Voidian.

ACKNOWLEDGEMENTS

To Oscar Ichazo, the Father of the Modern Day Enneagram
which he calls the Enneagon.
To the memory of Alfred Korzybski, the Father
of General Semantics.
To Allen Horne for his excellent editorial services.

To my Divine Leni

THE AUTHOR

Stephen H. Wolinsky, Ph.D., began his clinical practice in Los Angeles, California in 1974. A Gestalt and Reichian therapist and trainer, he led workshops in Southern California. He was also trained in Classical Hypnosis, Psychosynthesis, Psychodrama/Psychomotor, and Transactional Analysis. In 1977 he journeyed to India, where he lived for almost six years studying meditation. He moved to New Mexico in 1982 to resume a clinical practice. There he began to train therapists in Ericksonian Hypnosis and family therapy. Dr. Wolinsky also conducted year-long trainings entitled: "Integrating Hypnosis with Psychotherapy," and "Integrating Hypnosis with Family Therapy."

Dr. Wolinsky is the author of *Trances People Live: Healing Approaches in Quantum Psychology®*, *Quantum Consciousness: The Guide to Experiencing Quantum Psychology®*, *The Tao of Chaos: Quantum Consciousness Volume II*, *The Dark Side of the Inner Child*; and *Hearts on Fire: The Roots of Quantum Psychology*. He has recently completed a trilogy, *The Way of the Human: The Quantum Psychology Notebooks*. He is the founder of Quantum Psychology® and lives in Capitola, California. Dr. Wolinsky can be reached for workshop information by calling (831) 464-0564 or by FAX at (831) 479-8233.

TABLE OF CONTENTS •••

A person is three things:
what he thinks he is
what others think he is,
and
what he *really* <u>is.</u>

Anonymous

INTRODUCTION •••

Over the last several years, there have been many requests for a book that made Quantum Psychology more accessible for readers who are unfamiliar with it. I thought possibly of a Quantum Psychology primer or maybe something along the lines of the *Lazy Man's Guide to Enlightenment*. This seemed *right-on* since for years people have been calling me lazy. My reply had always been, "I'm not lazy, I'm mature." And simply put, Quantum Psychology is about maturity. Being mature enough to look at ourselves and take responsibility for our decisions and their consequences so we can go beyond ourselves and who we think we are.

What these requests did was give me an opportunity to pick and choose from some 3,000 pages of published material—what was essential and a must, and what was less important. In short, putting down a clear, concise context for Quantum Psychology, omitting extraneous details and demonstrations, and featuring some of what I consider to be *Quantum Psychology's Greatest Hits*.

The project was not difficult, but rather a nuts and bolts overview. My goal was to simplify Quantum Psychology, whose purpose is the realization of **Who You Are** by realizing that you are beyond anything you think or imagine yourself to be—and ultimately realizing that there is no "I" or beyond.

So, here goes **NOTHING**. Enjoy the ride.

With love
Your Brother, Stephen
September 1999

SECTION I •••

THE CONTEXT OF QUANTUM PSYCHOLOGY

Finding out **WHO YOU ARE** is not about being more, doing more, having more, manifesting more, creating more, being the best you can be, finding out your imagined mission or purpose in life, or having financial success.

Finding out **WHO YOU ARE** is the realization that everything is made of the same substance, and **YOU ARE THAT ONE SUBSTANCE**.

THE ADVAITA VEDANTA OF IT

THE CONTEXT OF QUANTUM PSYCHOLOGY

In India, there are two major approaches to self-realization, *Advaita* and *Vedanta*. *Advaita*, or non-dual awareness, means that there's only one substance, not two or more substances, in other words, *non-duality*. The most workable definition of *Vedanta* can best be expressed as, realizing who you are through discarding all you think or imagine yourself to be. In short, *not this/not this* or *neti-neti* in Sanskrit. The Vedas are considered the most sacred texts of India. Vedanta means the end of the Vedas.

THE PURPOSE OF QUANTUM PSYCHOLOGY

Quantum Psychology is different from other forms of modern-day psychology because it has a different purpose and a different aim, that of discovering **WHO YOU ARE**. The preliminary and preparatory stages are developed by dismantling (*neti-neti*) what is called your False Core-False Self and acquiring multi-dimensional awareness. We'll be discussing what all these terms mean as we go along.

Quantum Psychology is not intended to make you better, more virtuous, teach you how to have great relationships, how to make more money, or even how to feel more comfortable in your life. Rather, it is concerned with developing awareness so that you can discover **Who You Are**, even beyond awareness itself.

Multi-Dimensional Awareness is the developing of the consciousness of eight dimensions or manifestations of awareness. Quantum Psychology considers that the development of multi-dimensional awareness *might* help in the process of discovering **WHO YOU ARE**. Incidentally, I always say *might* since there can be no guarantees.

I lived in India for six years where I studied with many teachers, gurus and meditation masters. In 1979, I met Sri Nisargadatta Maharaj who was to become my teacher and spiritual mentor. According to him, "The only way to find out **Who You Are** is to find out **Who You Are Not**" (*neti-neti*). Nisargadatta Maharaj's most basic Quantum Psychology Principle: was: "Anything that you think you are, you are not." While he was alive, only one of his books was published, *I Am That*, which could arguably be called one of the most important spiritual texts of this generation. He was into *Advaita-Vedanta*, and *Jnana Yoga*. Jnana yoga is the Sanskrit term for the path of knowledge. Actually it is the PATH OF UNLEARNING (*neti-neti*), or as in *Star Wars* when Yoda (the teacher) says to Luke Skywalker (the student), "You must unlearn all that you have learned." Advaita contends that there is only **ONE SUBSTANCE**, that everything is made of **THAT ONE SUBSTANCE**, not two or more substances, and that spirituality is really about the realization that you are **THAT ONE SUBSTANCE**. According to the Maharaj:

In the beginning there was **NOTHING**, absolutely. The **I AM** appeared (condensed) within that **NOTHINGNESS**. And one day, the **I AM** will disappear (thin-out) and there will be **NOTHING** again and that is all it is.

QUANTUM PSYCHOLOGY AND NISARGADATTA MAHARAJ

"Personality is a mis-taken identity."
Nisargadatta Maharaj

Because of Nisargadatta Maharaj's influence, Quantum Psychology is directed toward enquiry and dismantling who you think or imagine yourself to be. The process is organized through a process of *enquiry*. In Quantum Psychology, we want to reduce the amount of awareness placed on, and consumed by, your *psychology*, in this way liberating your awareness until the enquir<u>er</u>-enquir<u>ee</u> and the awar<u>er</u> and awareness themselves disappear in the non-dimensionality of the underlying unity of **THAT ONE SUBSTANCE**.

Quantum Psychology is thus a by-product and continuation of Nisargadatta Maharaj and of **ADVAITA VEDANTA**, with the following basic core Quantum Psychology Principles:

ADVAITA: THE BOTTOM LINE

There is only **THAT ONE SUBSTANCE**. Not two or more substances

VEDANTA: THE PROCESS
NETI-NETI (Not This-Not This)

THE CORE OF QUANTUM PSYCHOLOGY

The Nine Quantum Psychology Principle:s of Nisargadatta Maharaj

1. There is only **ONE SUBSTANCE**.
2. What you know about yourself came from outside of you, therefore discard it.
3. Question everything, do not believe anything.
4. In order to find out **Who You Are**, you must first find out **Who You Are** not.

5. In order to let go of something, you must first know what it is.
6 The experienc_er_ is contained within the experience itself.
7. Anything you think you are—you are NOT.
8. Hold onto the **I AM**, let go of everything else.
9. Anything you know about you can not be.

These nine Quantum Psychology Principles form the core of Quantum Psychology.

THE I AM

Now, before we go much further, I would like to give you an explanation of what Nisargadatta meant when he said, "Hold on to the **I AM** and let go of everything else."

Prior to the arising of any thoughts, "you" were there in the No-state state of **I AM**. When thoughts, feelings, or whatever, arise, this Stateless state is still there. When thoughts and associations leave, the No-state state is there. That is the meaning of, "Hold on to the **I AM** and let go of anything else."

To experience this, let your eyes close and notice what occurs *if you do not use your thoughts, memories, emotions, associations, perceptions, attention, or intentions* That blankness is prior to thought. When Nisargadatta Maharaj said, "Anything you think you are, you are not," he meant that you existed "prior" to your thoughts, memory, emotion, associations, perceptions, attention, or intentions, in the Stateless State or the No-State State of the non-verbal **I AM**.

In order to get in touch with this state, you need to take your attention away from how you normally access information. By not using thoughts memory, emotion, associations, perceptions, attention, or intentions, notice a blankness which is naturally there. In the beginning you may only be able to experience this blankness for an instant since everything you normally use is put aside. The more often you are in this stateless state, the deeper and longer will these instants that the **I Am** will occur. For now, it is more important to begin to notice what exists prior to your thoughts, memory, emotion, associations, perceptions, attention, or intentions.

EXERCISE, THE I AM: THE FIRST STEP

(HAVE A FRIEND GUIDE YOU THROUGH THIS ONE)

Let your eyes close for a moment.

Without using your thoughts, memories, emotions, associations, perceptions, attention, or intentions, are you a man, a woman, or neither?

Without using your thoughts, your memory, your emotions, your associations, perceptions, attention, or intentions, are you limited, unlimited or neither?

Without using your thoughts, memory, emotion, associations, perceptions, attention, or intentions, are you defined, undefined, or neither?

Without using your thoughts, memory, emotion, associations, perceptions, attention, or intentions, what is healing?

Without using your thoughts, memories, emotions, associations, perceptions, attention, or intentions, what is it that needs to be healed?

Without using your thoughts, memories, emotions, associations, perceptions, attention, or intentions, what does existence or non-existence even mean or does it have any meaning at all?

Without using your thoughts, memory, emotions, associations, perceptions, attentions or intentions, *notice* the sound of one hand clapping.

Now, in a moment I'm (the guide) going to ask you to open your eyes and come back to the room, while leaving part of your awareness in the *No-state state of no thoughts, memory, emotion, associations*, perceptions, attention, or intentions. When you open your eyes, part of your awareness can notice the No-State state of no thoughts, memories, emotions, associations, perceptions, attention, or intentions; while another part of your awareness can be back here in this room. So whenever you are ready, let your eyes open. . . .

Welcome to the
Stateless State of
I AM

2 ● ● ●

THE QUANTUM OF IT

> *The observer cannot be separated from*
> *that which is observed.*
> Werner Heisenberg

> *Everything is emptiness, form is condensed emptiness.*
> Albert Einstein

> *Nothingness is the building block of the universe.*
> John Wheeler

> *The universe is an interconnected whole.*
> David Bohm

> *There are no local causes*
> John Stuart Bell

Twenty five hundred years before Einstein said that *everything was made of* **EMPTINESS,** *and that form was condensed* **EMPTINESS**, Buddha wrote in the *Heart Sutra* that *"Form is none other than* **EMPTINESS** *is none other than form."* But what does this mean and how can we examine it? Imagine that you were able to look into the quantum world. If you could, *you would not see* solid chairs or people, or any of the things you take for granted. Instead, you would see **EMPTINESS**, with a few particles that appeared to be floating in it. To illustrate how much **EMPTINESS** there is, imagine that an electron spinning around the nucleus of an atom were the earth and the nucleus around which it spins the sun. If this were the case, the space between the electron and the nucleus would be many times greater than the actual distance that is between the real earth and the real sun. That's how much **EMPTINESS** there is. So though everything *appears* solid through our normal, everyday lens or nervous system, actually things are very, very **EMPTY.**

In the same way, discovering **Who You Are** and the underlying unity of **THAT EMPTINESS** can *hopefully* be aided by dismantling the lenses frames of reference and concepts by which you view the world and yourself. And in this way, the underlying unity of **THAT ONE SUBSTANCE**, which is **Who You Are**, can then be realized.

3 • • •

THE BUDDHISM OF IT

Where does Buddhism fit into Quantum Psychology? Or perhaps this chapter should be called Everything you wanted to know about Buddhism but were afraid to ask? As you can see in the following, there is a great deal of overlap between Quantum Psychology and Buddhism. Here are some basic premises of Buddhist thought:

1) "Emptiness is none other than form—form none other than emptiness."

2) One who seeks Nirvana is ignorant—one who seeks Samsara is ignorant. Why? Because since there is only **ONE SUBSTANCE**, Nirvana is Samsara/Samsara is Nirvana.

3) There is no individual, separate soul which transmigrates or incarnates from lifetime to lifetime. Why? Because there is only **ONE SUBSTANCE**, therefore, no separate individual souls or self—just one *soul* or *substance*.

4 ●●●

THE BIOLOGY OF IT

WHY WE DON'T "GET" THE UNDERLYING UNITY OF EMPTINESS

The reason the world appears to be solid is because the nervous system makes things appear that way. Moshe Feldenkrais said, "The purpose of the nervous system is to organize chaos." The nervous system takes the alleged chaos of **EMPTINESS** and organizes it into what we see as the world and ourself. But prior to this organization, *everything is* **EMPTINESS** *Form is condensed emptiness*, and there is only **ONE SUBSTANCE**.

Quantum Psychology is not a quick fix or cure all, there are no guarantees.

Quantum Psychology is not for everybody. There are some people for whom it really, really works. For others it doesn't.

Quantum Psychology *hopes* that multi-dimensional awareness as a vehicle that *might* help you discover **Who You Are**. Note that *might* is underlined since there are no guarantees nor can any individual promise that there will be.

Ultimately, even the individual doing the process, along with awareness itself, disappears as you find out **Who You Are** by finding out **Who You Are Not**, in this way even the *who* evaporates.

5 ● ● ●

DEVELOPING MULTI-DIMENSIONAL AWARENESS

THE DIMENSIONS OF MANIFESTATION AND AWARENESS MADE SIMPLE

External Dimension
|
Thinking Dimension
|
Emotional Dimension
|
Biological-Animal Dimension

ESSENCE
|
I AM
|
COLLECTIVE UNCONSCIOUS
|
NOT-I-I

****
VOID
|
NAMELESS ABSOLUTE
|
THE BEYOND

EIGHT DIMENSIONS

As a beginning step and a possible aid in the discovery of **Who You Are**, Quantum Psychology first looks toward the liberation of awareness through the development of multi-dimensional awareness. To paraphrase noted Sufi master Idries Shah, You cannot become free until you have volitional choice over where you place your awareness. If your awareness is unknowingly fixated on re-enacting, reinforcing, resisting or re-creating through the False Self in an attempt to overcome the False Core, it can be difficult to experience freedom (to be discussed later) especially in the case of *spiritualization*, which is a defense in which situations are seen as "spiritual" in order to avoid dealing with unwanted feelings or thoughts about what is really going on. Developing awareness of the eight dimensions of manifestation and appreciating what each level does, its function and purpose, is essential for the liberation of awareness and the subjective experience of freedom.

In the chapters which follow, there will be a description of each dimension with an in-depth explanation that includes examples and exercises. These eight dimensions of manifestation will be discussed throughout the book since they provide a foundation to the understanding of Quantum Psychology.

There are eight dimensions of awareness and three levels which are beyond awareness: 1) the External Dimension; 2) the Thinking Dimension; 3) the Emotional Dimension; 4) the Biological-Animal Dimension; 5) **ESSENCE**; 6) the **I AM**; 7) the **COLLECTIVE UNCONSCIOUS**; and 8) the **NOT-I-I**. The three levels beyond are: 1) the **VOID**; 2) the **NAMELESS ABSOLUTE** and 3) the **BEYOND**

Fourth Way teacher, G. I. Gurdjieff, once told his well-known student, P. D. Ouspensky (1949),

16

When I pay attention to the external world, I am like an arrow pointing outward. When I close my eyes and sink into myself, my attention becomes an arrow pointing inwards. Now, if I try to do both at once—to point the arrow in and out at the same time—I immediately discover that this is incredibly difficult. After a second or two, I either forget the outside world and sink into a daydream, or forget myself and become absorbed in what I am looking at.

Gurdjieff called this 'self remembering'. Quantum Psychology asks that you learn to focus on three or more dimensions simultaneously. In order to do this, you need to understand the inherent qualities of each dimension and how these qualities function in your life.

CONFUSING THE LEVELS

A Sufi Master was visiting a village and one of his students decided to see him. The student rode for miles across the desert until he reached the little village. But when he got there, he couldn't find a place to tie up his camel. He was so eager that he simply left the camel behind and went to where the guru was staying. They spoke for a couple of hours until it was time for the guru to leave. Then, realizing the student's camel was nowhere to be seen, the Sufi master asked him, "Where's your camel?" "I couldn't find a place to tie him up so I left it to God to take care of him," the student said. The Sufi master replied, "That's good, you should leave everything to God. *And tie up your camel.*" This is a classic example of confusing or trying to use one dimension (the **VOID**) to handle another dimension (the External World). So, yes. Leave everything to God. But don't forget to tie up your camel.

Each of the eight dimension has a different function. The purpose of my right hand is to write, the purpose of my mouth is to eat. I cannot digest my food by holding it in my hand. And I can't write by putting my pen in my mouth. It's not functional. In this way, you need to know the function of each dimension. Simply put, the more dimensions of awareness available to you, the greater your subjective experience of freedom. The less dimensions you are aware of, the less will be your subjective experience of freedom.

17

Confusing one level for another is a classic New Age problem. For example, some people imagine that by visualizing money coming to them, money will magically appear. I have never met anyone who actually made money this way. When I first came back from India, I shared an office with a man from Los Angeles who led workshops for visualizing money. The problem was he couldn't pay his rent. In this way, he was confusing the thinking world (the world of mental images) with the external world. If I fantasize myself being an astronaut, it has nothing to do with my being one in the external world. It's a fantasy and, though true at a thinking image level, at the external level it is not true.

> ## QUANTUM PSYCHOLOGY PRINCIPLE:
> What is true at one level is not necessarily true at another level. When one level of awareness is confused with another, it can cause problems.

6 •••

THE FALSE CORE-
FALSE SELF

We are not afraid of experiences, we are only afraid
of what we have concluded that experiences mean.
Stephen H. Wolinsky

Before we go too much further, let us begin by creating a context for where we are headed. In other words, we need to explain
the False Core-False Self and how it functions in our lives.

QUANTUM PSYCHOLOGY PRINCIPLE:

Anything you think you are, you are not. Anything you
think or imagine yourself to be, you are beyond. Because
you name something doesn't mean you know it. You only
know the name you gave it. In the same way, the ideas
which you conclude about a thing are not the thing you are
referring to.

In order to stabilize awareness, the False Core-False Self must
be processed, understood, digested, and liberated. The False Core-
is the one concept, the one assumption, you hold about yourself,
which organizes your entire psychology. It represents the "you"

you call yourself, how you see the world, how you imagine the world sees you, and how you see yourself. It is the glue which holds this "you" together. The False Self is how you attempt to hide, heal, and in a word, *compesnsate*, for the False Core. Any attempt at compensation only reinforces the False Core-False Self which is holographic and is one unit.

AN OVERVIEW OF THE FALSE CORE

The False Core is that one conclusion that you have about yourself which holds your entire psychology together and organizes not only your every thought, emotion, action, fantasy, and reaction, etc., but also how you imagine others see you. In *Trances People Live* (1986), I call this the *Organizing Principle.* Since the False Core organizes our view of the world, our view of ourselves, and how we imagine the world views us, along with an emotional component, I would like to begin this section with some general comments about its meaning.

It is crucial to explore the False Core conclusion because if you believe in a false premise, then all of the premises which follow must also be false. It's as if you were building a house on shifting sands and were trying to compensate for this weak foundation by using bricks of either psychology or spirituality to make it stable. Because it is not supported solidly in the ground, it will flounder at the least change in weather (external context).

According to Freud, "All traumas come in chains of earlier, similar events." This statement suggests that everything in our personality structure is organized and associated in what *appears* to itself to be similar, thus creating a pattern. It can be said that for survival reasons, the nervous system has a generalizing function. For example, "All men are *fill in the blank*," "All women are *fill in the blank*," "All relationships are *fill in the blank*," "All races are *fill in the blank*," etc.

The nervous system creates the illusion that things, events, or people are similar and then *over generalizes*, making them appear the same when they are not. This survival mechanism is built into the nervous system. Remember the famous zen saying;

You never put your foot in the same river twice. . . .

QUANTUM PSYCHOLOGY PRINCIPLE:

The False Core conclusion can only lead to more False conclusions and to more False solutions because the conclusions and solutions are not based in present time reality. And the solutions are based on a False conclusion.

DISMANTLING THE FALSE CORE

To discover **WHO YOU ARE**, it *might* be helpful if the False Core-False Self is dismantled.

Quantum Psychology studies the False Core to demonstrate the organization of the personality which, in turn, leads us to understand *who we thought we were but are not*. Remember, the purpose of Quantum Psychology is to find out **WHO YOU ARE**. The purpose of discovering your False Core-False Self is to find out *who you imagine you are*—but are actually not and then discarding it (*neti-neti*). In this way, as Nisargadatta Maharaj said, "you can find out who you are by first finding out who you are not." In this process, we develop the Eight Dimensions of Awareness, the **VOID** and the **NAMELESS ABSOLUTE**, being beyond dimensions and beyond Quantum Psychology.

The False Core is invisible to you because you think it *is* you. For example, "I always feel inadequate," "I always feel worthless" or "I always feel alone," are False Cores which are never questioned because they are so interwoven into the fabric of "you" and "your" life that you do not see them. They are transparent, like looking through a glass of which you are unaware. In the same way, you see the world and yourself through this pane (pain) of glass, this lens or frame, which you think is you, without realizing it is a lens.

The False Core is the one concept, the one belief, the one conclusion, the one structure, that you have drawn about yourself. It organizes your entire psychological frame.

You only have one False Core, but you have an infinite number of ways of defending against it. Defending means trying to overcome it or resist it in some way.

Freud's simple and yet profound concept of chains of earlier similar events is a cornerstone of modern-day psychology. It is a concept which Quantum Psychology finds extremely useful in dealing with the False Core, this tendency of the mind and the nervous system to organize and over generalize events into similar categories or patterns. In Quantum Psychology we call this organizational tendency the *Associational Trance.*

ORIGIN AND MEANING OF
THE FALSE CORE

IN THE BEGINNING

How does the False Core develop? To appreciate this, we can use the *lens* or *story* of Psychoanalytic Developmental Psychology, understanding that it too is a lens we are looking through, a point of view, or a map or model of what is although it is *not what is.* To explain, psychoanalytic research theorizes that newborn children believe that they and their mother are one, and that between 5-12 months, infants realize that they are separate from their mother.

Quantum Psychology theorizes that the False Core is the false reason or false conclusion children draw to explain why they are separate. In this way, the False core provides the infant with a *False Cause.* Once the *False Cause* is believed, the mind creates a False solution or False Self to overcome this fantasized *False Cause.* This trauma of separation is called the *narcissistic wound* or *narcissistic injury.* Upon this realization of being separate, the **I AM** is formed and the False Core conclusion provides a *False Cause* as to why you are separate. Quantum Psychology defines narcissism as, "I am the source and center of the universe," "My mother and I are one," "I created it all." Later narcissism can become, "I must make mother my reflection," "I must reflect back to her what I imagine she wants so she will reflect me (be my reflection)," etc., etc., etc. This *False Cause* conclusion is the False Core. The *solution* to this False Core (Cause) is based on a False conclusion, hence, it is a False solution. And from this False Core Cause conclusion, a False Self solution emerges to hide, overcome, transform, heal, resist, deny, and in a word, *overcome* or *overcompensate* for the False Core. Once solidified, the False Core-False Self seals your psycho-emotional and even your spiritual fate.

THE FALSE CORE—FALSE SELF MADE EASY

When you realize you are separate from your mother, there is a traumatic shock, the **I AM** along with the False Core-False Self is solidified. You then spend the rest of your life dealing with the trauma by trying to overcome it, heal it, resist it, hide it, resolve it, transform it, or spiritualize it. The conclusion or *False Cause* drawn from this separation is what Quantum Psychology calls the False Core—which you continually try to overcome in some way. Always remember, the False Core is a concept, a *False Cause* which you believe is real; and so any solution based on a False conclusion can only yield further False conclusions and False solutions. For this reason, because the False Self is a concept which occurs after the False Core and is based on the earlier False conclusion, it is more false than the False Core itself.

It should be noted that in psychology, if a client comes in with the problem of "I am worthless," it is assumed that this is truly the problem. Then, steps are taken to work this out. In Quantum Psychology, the concept of "I am worthless" is defined as a False conclusion about why something happened, which you cannot heal because it is false, a false reason. You must see the False conclusion for what it is, a False conclusion—and discard it.

QUANTUM PSYCHOLOGY PRINCIPLE:

Any treatment aimed at transforming or changing the False Core is organized by the False Self and is based on believing in the False conclusion. Hence, the therapy or spiritual practice can only yield poor, if any results.

THE NARCISSISTIC WOUND OR INJURY

When children experience themselves as separate from mom, the shock to the nervous system causes a narcissistic wound or injury. At the moment of this shock, an infant's *False Core* begins to solidify. This False Core is what they conclude about themselves and their separation from Mom. Thus a *False Cause* is attributed to this natural separation process. Examples include, "I am separate *because* I'm worthless," "I am separate *because* I'm inadequate," "I am separate *because* I don't exist," "I am separate *because* I'm powerless," and many others. As a result of their False Core conclusion, people might spend the rest of their lives acting it out in order prove that it is true or, if they are compensated by the False Self, trying to overcome it or prove it is not true.

How does the False Self attempt to resist the False Core? The False Self might try to overcome the False Core, heal the False Core, hide the False Core, spiritualize the False Core, transform the False Core, or justify the False Core, etc.—all of these are handled by your False Self in its role as compensator.

Though the False Core solidifies due to the shock of the Realization of Separation, prior to this, it existed in a latent form. It appears to have an energetic-genetic proclivity, which runs in families, such as cancer, diabetes or heart disease. There is no choice involved because that would imply you can choose your own genetic proclivities. The very idea of such a choice is narcissistic and reflects the infantile grandiosity behind such statements as, "I create it all," "I chose my parents," "I am responsible for everything."

This energetic-genetic predisposition can be likened to what Homeopathic medicine calls a *miasm*. If your grandfather had tuberculosis, for example, then you would have a proclivity toward that disease though your symptoms might only be a runny nose when it rains. Homeopathic doctors could try to make this link by analyzing your genetic lineage. In the same way the False Core - False Self has a energetic-genetic lineage.

The False Core-False Self is also called the False Core *Driver*-False Self *Compensator*. This emphasizes their distinct roles, namely, that the False Core *drives* your psychology while the False Self tries to *compensate* for what it mistakes as your lack.

THE DYNAMICS OF
THE FALSE CORE–FALSE SELF

In a very simple way, we can say that on a neurological level, the brain and nervous system organize in the following order: 1) There is a bodily sensation. 2) Another part of the brain registers and acknowledges the sensation. 3) The sensation is then labeled as sadness, fear, happiness, anger, etc. 4) Then, from another level, the brain says, "Sadness is bad," or "Happiness is good." 5) On yet another level, the brain says, "I should change sadness into happiness, I should do something about it."

Each time you move up a level, you get further away from what *is*. You move away from your basic sensation, which is what is, to the cortical level of your brain, which is defining what it is. In other words, as you move from the label of sensation (1) to sad-

24

ness (3), millions of stimuli are omitted and a few are selected out by the nervous system and brain to draw this particular conclusion. In this way, you move further away from *what is*, as the nervous system chooses what information to use and draws more conclusions about why what is, is. Furthermore, the labeling of sensation occurs after the experience has already happened, and the nervous system's label omits and selects out so much information, and it only justifies sensations or action, thus coming up with reasons about what is, which are untrue. The False Core conclusion, therefore, since it omits much more than it takes in, is not even close to what really is. It is a map, an idea of what is—not what is.

In this way, Alfred Korzysbski, the noted father of general semantics said, "The map is not the territory," "the idea is not the thing it is referring to."

THE MAJOR FALSE CORE-FALSE SELFS'

Following is a list of the major False Core-False Selves. There might be a tendency to jump in and say, "This is me" or "That is definitely not what I do." But it takes time to figure out your False Core-False Self since often it's *what you don't know which actually drives your psychology, as opposed to what you do know.*

FALSE CORE	FALSE SELF
1. "There must be something wrong with me."	Prove there is *not* "something wrong with me" and act "as if" I am perfect.
2. "I am worthless."	Prove I am *not* worthless and act as if I have value or worth.
3. "I cannot do."	Prove or act "as if" I am an over-achiever.
4. "I am inadequate."	Prove I am not inadequate and act "as if" I am overly adequate.
5. "I don't exist."	Prove or act "as if" I exist or am something.
6. "I am alone."	Prove or act "as if" I am connected.
7. "I am incomplete."	Prove I am *not* incomplete and act "as if" I feel complete.
8. "I am powerless."	Prove I am *not* powerless and act "as if" I am powerful.
9. "I am loveless."	Prove I am *not* loveless and act "as if" I am lovable.

Please note: Quantum Psychology uses "as if" because it is an integrated *act* or *pretend* of the False Self and hence it is not real.

25

HOW DOES THE FALSE CORE-FALSE SELF FUNCTION?

Your False Core-False Self is a lens, a trance , a frame of reference, through which you view the world and yourself, and also how you imagine the world views you. In this way, the False Core of, say, "I am worthless" or "I am inadequate," will interpret every situation through its lens or trance.

Each False Core-False Self interprets life through its own particular lens. If three people get in a car accident, one might say, "I'm worthless, that's why it happened." Another might feel a deep sense of powerlessness and still a third might feel, "What's wrong with me? I should have taken driving lessons." In other words, each False Core has interpreted the same trauma through three different lenses and gives three different reasons, stories, or justifications for what is. If you could take off the lens or not have a frame of reference, if you could dismantle the False Core, you would feel the ease and flow of life and *naturally* experience **ESSENCE** and the **I AM**.

To take this a step further, I am often asked, "Why are **ESSENCE** and **I AM** not available?" The reason they go unnoticed or are not stabilized in our awareness is because most of our attention is knowingly or unknowingly focused on the False Core. At the same time we are continually trying to somehow overcome it through False Self Compensator. Any attempt to reform the False Core, transform it, reframe it, re-associate it, take the good, healthy stuff and leave the bad unhealthy stuff, turn our vices into virtues, etc.—all are strategies of the False Self Compensator which tries to overcome, resist and resolve the False Core. As you can see, the False Self can be extremely insidious. Also, it is important to remember that the False Core-False Self is one holographic unit; you can't have one without the other.

The False Core always wins, it always re-enforces itself. In other words, if your False Core is "I am worthless," no matter how much you give to others to try to feel a sense of worth, deep down you always feel worthless. If your False Core is "I am inadequate," no matter how much you try to prove how adequate you are, deep down you still feel inadequate. What compounds the problem is that **ESSENCE** and the **I AM** become involved in the shock and get mixed together with the False Core. After the shock of the Realization of Separation trauma, you conclude that it was caused by

ESSENCE- I AM, which is then mis-labeled, and its Essential quality of **Spaciousness** is now seen as emptiness, as a lack.

And so we deny and resist our **ESSENCE- I AM** (the State-less State) because it is fused with the shock of the Realization of Separation and the False Core, and thus we blame and want to get rid of it. In order to grow the awareness of **ESSENCE,** it requires freeing up the awareness which is unknowingly fixated on the False Core-False Self. Once we realize that the False Core-False Self is an attempt to organize and resist the chaos resulting from the shock of the Realization of Separation, and are willing to go through that, our narcissistic wound begins to heal, everything shifts, our fixation on the False Core-False Self begins to soften, and **ESSENCE-I AM** moves into our awareness. This is a major awakening.

Because of the False Core, results in therapy are often poor because you believe in this *False Cause* and hence you try to heal a *False Cause, fantasized reason, a false story* which was made-up by the nervous system after the fact to justify and organize the shock of the Realization of Separation. Furthermore, the False Self is oftentimes re-enforced in therapy as it is strengthened to resist the False Core. "Therapy" is sometimes centered around creating a False Self Compensator to attempt to hide, overcome, resist, heal, cope, handle, or transform this mistaken, infantile conclusion about the shock of the Realization of Separation. In this process, **ES-SENCE** is denied while, ironically, at the same time, the False Self is constantly searching for a False solution to the False Core conclusion. This searching by the False Self only re-enforces the False Core-False Self, which needs to be experienced as false in order for **ESSENCE-I AM** to be realized.

If the lens or frame of reference of the False Core-False Self does not end, it will continue to be acted out. That was the piece of the puzzle which I finally discovered while I was living in India. Let's say my father was an alcoholic and to try to transcend that, I do mantras, yantras, and tantras—or whatever. I can have a beauti-ful meditation and a beautiful experience of the **VOID**. But the minute I open my eyes and come back to the external world, I'm right back with my *uncooked seeds* (see below) and all that they entail. Soon I am arguing with my spouse, bickering with my fa-ther, etc.

UNCOOKED SEEDS

In India, the metaphor of seeds is oftentimes used. If I have seeds and I plant and water them, I will soon have a plant which bears fruit. But if I first cook the seeds in a frying pan and then plant them, they won't grow or bear fruit. In this scenario, the seeds are symbols of your unprocessed, psychological material, the False Core-False Self. Awareness is the heat that cooks uncooked seeds (repressed, unprocessed) concepts. Thus, Quantum Psychology uses awareness to cook the uncooked seeds (beliefs, frames of reference, concepts, points of view, etc.) so that they no longer sprout and produce their poisonous fruit, and **ESSENCE-I AM** can become more available because attention is no longer unconsciously placed upon the False Core—False Self.

Many people who are trying to transcend their psychology are in a spiritual denial. They use meditation as medication because they don't want to feel things. In this way often-times transcendence becomes a defensive trance and a resistance which justifies spiritual philosophies. Simply put:

You cannot meditate your False Core-False Self away.
You cannot mantra your False-False Self away.
You have to be willing to look at and acknowledge everything that is there. Or as Nisargadatta Maharaj said, "You cannot let go of something until you know what it is."

Without dismantling the False Core-False Self you cannot expect to stabilize in **ESSENCE, I AM**.

SOME EXAMPLES OF DIFFERENT FALSE CORES

Let us now look at all of this through the eyes of different False Core Drivers and False Self Compensators.

Let's say at age five, a child is molested:

One False Core would say, "There's something wrong with me, that's the reason this happened."

Another False Core would say, "I'm worthless, even Uncle Henry is treating me as if I'm worthless.

Another False Core would probably get totally frozen and be unable to do anything about it. Later, through the False Self, they might become over-achievers to try to compensate for, or heal, their paralyzed inability to do.

Another False Core would say, "I was molested and it really means I'm incredibly inadequate. It's my own fault, I screwed up."

Another False Core would dissociate. "After all, I am nothing, I have nothing, I don't even exist, Maybe nothing happened." They have split off from the emotional dimension associated with the event. Later they might spiritualize it. A recent book came out which both spiritualized and re-framed molestation as a gift from God, an opportunity. But these spiritual re-frames deny the pain of molestation.

Another False Core might think, "This means I'm alone."

Another False Core might say, "I'm incomplete, I'm not enough. If only I were enough, had more experiences, then it wouldn't have happened."

Another False Core might feel powerless. Interestingly, the "I am powerless" False Core often is resisted by the False Self saying, "Actually I wasn't molested. I seduced Uncle Henry."

Another False Core might say, "See, I knew there was no love in the world."

HEALING THE FALSE CORE-FALSE SELF: WHO IS IN THE DRIVER'S SEAT?

In the process of going beyond the False Core-False Self, the False Self tries to overcome the False Core and the *False Cause* or reason for the shock—which is not the shock itself. It is an insidious attempt by the False Self to heal or transform the False Core since it is still an attempt to overcome or compensate for it. The False Self is part of the False Core, it appears later than the False Core and since it is based or emerges from the False Core conclusion, it is more false than the False Core. It is the False Self which tries to overcome the False Core. Why is the False Self unable to heal or overcome the False Core? The False Core-False Self is one unit, like inhaling and exhaling, and you can't have one without the other. That's why I prefer the descriptions of each False Core-False Self to focus on the False Core since it is less compensated, closer to the experience, and demonstrates that which drives the machinery of your psychology.

Some psycho-spiritual schools believe that the False Self Compensator is healthier than the False Core. Quantum Psychology feels the opposite is true, that the compensator only gives the illusion of being healthier or more socially acceptable, but in reality it is an integrated age-regression, insidiously using the False Self as a defense against the False Core and the Realization of Separation. Until the False Self and its seductive, insidious nature is understood as an illusion, and an integrated age regression—and the discomfort felt and gone through—it is difficult to stabilize awareness in **ESSENCE-I AM** and **NOT-I-I**.

People respond to the False Core through the False Self by saying, "If only I didn't feel *fill in the blank*, everything would be fine." In this way they are always trying to get rid of the False Core by over compensation. For example, in order to handle the *fill in the blank*, "I'll take another lover. I'll make more money and then I won't be *fill in the blank*. If I have more experiences, then I'll be smart enough and I won't feel *fill in the blank*." These attempts to get rid of it, heal it, and transform it, are done by the False Self, and they only re-enforce the False Core, rather than just noticing, "Hey, here's my False Core of *fill in the blank*, isn't that interesting? I've organized my whole life around a concept which is not true!" If you can do this, you will soon see that it is only a concept—and an untrue concept at that.

The difficulty is that we must work with the False Core, *without the intention of getting rid of it.* You work with it to see what occurs. The question frequently is, "Doesn't there have to be an intention in order to process it in the first place?" No. If the processes are done from the Stateless State or No-State-State of **I AM**, there is no intention.

Next, study it and dismantle it until it can begin to fall away. You might see it, observe the associations, tracing back every thought, feeling and fantasy to see how your whole life has been organized around this one thing, and then dismantling it through enquiry. Ultimately, the enquiry continues until you realize that you are neither the enquirer, the questioner nor the answerer. But this understanding occurs much later when you see how everything is organized around this one structure. It is then that you can go beyond the obsessive-compulsive nature of the conceptual structure of the False Core, thus liberating your awareness.

Many spiritual systems attempt to deal with the False Core by saying that it can be overcome, healed or transformed. In doing so, they merely appeal to the seeker's False Self. These systems wind up creating spiritualized Archetypical stories, such as the fall of man, to explain and justify what is a natural, biological separation process—the shock of the Realization of Separation. It's not that these systems are, by their nature, bad; but they can re-enforce the False Core-False Self dyad.

When I was in India I spent some time with a popular teacher who had more than ten thousand disciples. I noticed that he gave the same mantra to everybody, offering a kind of *one size fits all* spirituality for all of his followers. I felt then and now that no two people are alike and each individual needs something tailored just for them; or, as Paul Simon sang, "One man's ceiling is another man's floor."

Many people are confused about "What is driving their psychology? What is the one concept that organizes everything in your life?" In Quantum Psychology, you learn to become clear about the False Core, and then trace all of your behavior back to it. This is an internal process, tracing your behavior, your actions, your feelings—in short, everything—back to your False Core. Once you get there, you will have to sit in it. There's no way around it. Do not try to change it. Anytime you try to change it or get rid of it, you are resisting it, which is one of the five strategies, or the five R's, of the False Self, namely, *re*-sisting, *re*-enacting, *re*-creating, *re*-enforcing and *re*-solving.

You must be willing to sit in your False Core and the shock of the Realization of Separation. Sitting in your False Core means you are free to and free not to BE or UN-BE it, but not to believe it, just to observe it *without trying to get rid of it.* Then, to go beyond it, you learn to be able to stay in the non-verbal **I AM** prior to it.

As Quantum Psychology said previously, every movement of your mind is driven by the False Core, and the interplay of the False Core-False Self. To paraphrase Nisargadatta Maharaj, Notice the ongoing contradictions within the mind (which is the False Core-False Self) and know they are not you. The movements of the mind are done to avoid the pain of the shock of the Realization of Separation and the False Core, which act as a *False Cause*, thus giving the False Self something to overcome so that it fantasizes that it can stay in control of their feelings and how others feel or see them. However, since the cause for the Realization of Separation is false, its solution too must be false. The False Core-False Self deprives you of the experience of **WHO YOU ARE**. Its obsessive-compulsive tendency eats away at your awareness of the

ESSENCE and **I AM**, (fantasized) which are blamed for the separation.

Once you understand this, you can begin to trace everything back from the False Self to the False Core and stay there until it dissolves.

THE FALSE CORE-FALSE SELF ENQUIRY

This might help to explain how this tracing process might proceed: Let's say I'm in my room in Oakland and I have a fantasy that I'm incredibly wealthy and live in Hawaii. I ask myself, If this dream doesn't come true, *what would be the worst of it? Or what's so bad about that?* Well, the worst part about not being rich and living in Maui is that I feel worthless. Then, I would continue with my enquiry: "So what's the worst part or so bad about feeling worthless?" I might respond, "Well no one would want to have anything to do with me and I would be alone." Continue the enquiry. Question: "What's the worst of being alone?" Response: "Well, I would have no love." Enquiry question: "What's the worst or so bad about having no love?" Response: "That's it!" The enquiry would continue until I reached bottom where ultimately I'd go, "That's it!"

Once you know what you're False Core is, you'll see that every fantasy you have—good, bad or indifferent—and everything that you're doing, can be traced back to your False Core. Now, between the False Core and the False Self there's a layer of amnesia because the False Self does not want to know that the False Core is there. But fortunately for us, no trance and no amnesia are fool-proof so the False Core is always leaking through. Thus, the False Self can never overcome the False Core, no matter what techniques are used. The problem is that attempts to transform or jump levels by going to another dimension and substituting love for anger play into the hands of the False Self, which is doing the work. Another problem is that the False Self is very tricky, so tricky, in fact, that you actually don't realize what's happening. You're seduced into believing that this time things are going to come out differently (and you will overcome the False Core); but, of course, everything always winds up exactly the same.

REVIEWING HOW TO GO BEYOND THE FALSE CORE–FALSE SELF DILEMMA

1) Acknowledge that the False Core exists.

2) Notice where it is in your body. Is it in your chest? Your heart?

3) Observe it, have it, step into it, be it 100 percent. Then, step out and observe it. The key is not to try to get rid of it. If you're trying to get rid of it, you're in the False Self. You have to be able to step in and out of it, and to observe it without trying to get rid of it. This develops the essential quality of acceptance.

4) Create it a few times.

5) Stay in the **I AM** (i.e., without using your thoughts, memories, emotions, associations, perceptions, attention, or intentions.

6) Begin to allow it to dismantle.

GOING BEYOND THE FALSE CORE

QUANTUM PSYCHOLOGY PRINCIPLE:

During the shock of the Realization of Separation, the False Core begins to solidify and, simultaneously, there occurs a loss of awareness of the **I AM** and **ESSENCE** .

To review, you can't go beyond the False Core until you acknowledge it, be it and to sit in it totally. When you are able to sit in your False Core, then you can move beyond and stabilize in your **ESSENCE** or **I AM**. But you have to know what pulls your chain of associations. I have seen students who try to overcome their False Core-False Self through meditation; and they might be able to sit in meditation and have an experience of **ESSENCE**, **I AM** or **NOT-I-I**; but when they open their eyes and go out into the world, you are going to get smacked in the face. For this reason, you have to be open to sitting in your False Core and the shock of the Realization of Separation and just experience what is there.

If you try to get out of it, it is always through resistance which only keeps the whole process going. So many systems of spirituality and psychotherapy fall into the False Self's trap by trying to maneuver you away from this False Core—even going so far as to ask you to keep the positive and leave the negative. The False Self in its role as compensator can be very seductive, which only serves to increase defensive resistance, re-enactment, and re-enforcement of the False Core.

But if you can observe your False Core–False Self without any intention of getting rid of it, then it is not an avoidance. Just ask yourself, "Am I observing the False Core to get rid of it, change it, heal it, or transform it? Or am I in the False Core to just observe it and notice what happens?"

BLOWING THE FALSE CORE

It is really important to realize that when the False Core blows, your personality, i.e., your thoughts, and feelings, will continue, but your False Core-False Self and your uncooked seeds will no longer have any subjective effect on you. So, even if there is an enormous amount going on in your external thinking, emotional and biological dimensions, when your False Core is blown—even in the midst of fear, pain, and anger—you will still feel unaffected with what is happening.

YOU ALWAYS TAKE YOUR FALSE CORE WITH YOU.

By observing someone's outward behavior, it is easy to imagine that you understand their False Core-False Self. But it's not that easy. You have to understand the motivation behind their behavior, and ask what drives their psychology? Let's say someone is studying biology. Are they studying because they "feel worthless and inadequate?" Or because "they don't want to be alone?" Do they "want to have power," or do they believe "there is something wrong with them?" These are difficult questions to answer, which is why it is hard to know what another's False Core is.

Always bear in mind that the False Core is not you, not your real core; but a concept through which you see the world and yourself, and by which you imagine the world sees you. And so, taking the False Core apart without the intention of getting rid of it, healing it, or transforming it, etc., is like taking the label off and having it as energy, (to be discussed later). The predicament is that, in order to avoid the separation wound, your nervous system is always re-creating your False Core; and at the same time, as an automatic survival response, trying to get rid of it or compensate for it through the False Self.

THE FALSE CORE DECONSTRUCTION PROCESS

Step 1. Acknowledge that there is a False Core-False Self.

Step 2. Own it.

Step 3. Un-own it. Get that it's not you.

Step 4. Dismantle it.

THE FALSE CORE-FALSE SELF AND ESSENCE-I AM

As mentioned previously, the **Spaciousness** of **ESSENCE-I AM** is mislabeled as empty (as in a lack) and blamed for the shock of the Realization of Separation. In other words, the reason or *False Cause* as to why I'm separate is because **ESSENCE-I AM** is so *fill in the False Core*. In this way, the Essential Quality of **Spaciousness** is mis-taken for a lack and resisted at a psychological level. Since **ESSENCE-I AM** is the only reference point prior to the separation, it is mistakenly assumed to have *caused* the trauma. With this concept in mind, you start splitting off from **ESSENCE-I AM**, thinking that it is bad. It becomes the disowned shadow. And the Essential Quality of **Spaciousness** is now mis-labeled as emptiness (as in a lack), and is then compensated for.

After **ESSENCE-I AM** is mis-labeled—the False Core becomes the reason and *False Cause* for the separation from your mother, such as, "There must be something wrong with me," etc. **ESSENCE** is now seen as a lack, and remains hidden from you. You need to realize that the False Core is the label placed on the (mis)labeled **Spaciousness** of **ESSENCE-I AM**. Once **ESSENCE**, is de-labeled, the Essential quality of **Spaciousness** arises.

DOES THE FALSE CORE COME BACK AFTER IT IS WORKED-OUT?

The answer is *yes*, under stress the False Core will come back. But as you become familiar with it, you will realize it and immediately discard it rather than acting it out. A student once asked Nisargadatta Maharaj, "Does anything ever come up for you?" "Every so often something comes up," he said, "but I *immediately* realize it's not me and discard it." So, it's important to recognize the False Self and be able to trace every thought, emotion, and fantasy, back to its source, the False Core.

GOING INTO THE I AM

The next step is to go into the non-verbal **I AM**, which exists prior to the False Core, so that you can see the False Core and its associations as *not you*. The more the False Core loses its impact on you, the more your psychology will no longer impact you. From the outside, other people might see you behaving in a certain way and interpret this as you being in your False Core. But internally and subjectively, you will remain unaffected. There is an old saying in Raja Yoga, "When a pick-pocket sees a saint, they only see their pockets." In this way, if someone is in their False Core-False Self, they only see their own and other people's False Core-False Self.

HOW TO WORK WITH
THE FALSE CORE-FALSE SELF

As mentioned before, the False Self comes into being as a defense against the False Core. That's the bad news. The good news is that you're not either of them. **You're not your False Core or your False Self**. They're just constructs, made-up concepts. Unfortunately, most people believe they're real, and they think that's who they are. But think of it like this: Before you took on your False Core, you were there in what was a no-state state, a Stateless State of no thoughts, memory, emotion, associations or perceptions. When you dismantle your False Core and it leaves, you will still be there. So, therefore, you can't be your False Core-False Self and when it is gone, the **I AM** is still there.

Notice any experience or thought that you're having right now. Now, prior to taking on that thought, simply stay there. The reason the False Core is so powerful is because all of your awareness and attention is *unknowingly* fixated on it, and you're always trying to overcome it. Now, when you meditate, you drop down somewhere into **ESSENCE–I AM**. When you open your eyes and come back, the False Core-False Self comes back, too.

When I lived in India I spent time with almost sixty different teachers, gurus, and meditation masters; but each time I would go into **ESSENCE-I AM** or **BEYOND**, it was only temporarily. Soon afterward, all my *stuff* would come back. I kept asking myself, after all the years I spent in India, why did this keep happening?

The gurus and teachers implicitly or explicitly that their systems would handle all my problems in all dimensions but that didn't happen.

I realized that different therapies or forms of meditation might be appropriate in one dimension but ineffective in another. I realized I had to deal with the False Core-False Self, which was obviously was more insidious than I thought. I had been in psychotherapy in the early 1970s, before I went to India, and I knew that I had to go back and take a look at what would handle this. As long as the False Core-False Self was operative, awareness in **ESSENCE-I AM** would never stabilize.

Just to illustrate, until the early 1970s, most gurus in India lived a pretty monastic life. They dwelled in small caves or obscure ashrams located in the middle of nowhere, and their needs were minimal. Then, they came to America or Europe, and their external context changed. Pretty soon, all of their uncooked seeds came up. All of a sudden, they wanted money, centers, fame, and lots of young women. Soon they tried to spiritualize (use spirituality to justify) their *uncooked seeds* by saying that they personally did not want meditation centers or money, that they were on a mission from God. It wasn't sex they personally wanted, it was Tantra. Everything used spirituality to justify (*spiritualization*), which was unsettling for students because there was a lie on top of what was really going on. Students then had to lie to themselves and age regress further because they couldn't manage what the guru (daddy or mommy) were doing.

> QUANTUM PSYCHOLOGY PRINCIPLE:
> Every time the external context changes, different aspects of the False Core arise.

HOW TO DISCOVER THE FALSE CORE

To determine your False Core and False Core Driver, take notice of whatever it is you are experiencing and then trace it back by asking yourself, *"What is the worst of that?"* or *"What is so bad about that?"* When you trace it back, you'll eventually hit the bottom of one of them.

> QUANTUM PSYCHOLOGY PRINCIPLE:
> Who you are is beyond the way you fixate your attention. The way you fixate attention, and all you call *you*, are part of the observer-False Core Driver-False Self Compensator Self Defensive complex.

TRAUMAS

The False Core has an associational component which acts like a filter through which all traumas are perceived, ordered and experienced. These traumas are then generalized to interpret different externals so that they match the False Core-False Self. Thus, *the False Core-False Self acts as a lens of interpretation as to what the trauma means to you.* Later it is used to interpret all subsequent experiences throughout your life.

In traumas especially there is a collapsing and confusing of the levels. Prior to trauma, everything is in motion—thoughts, memories, sensations, emotions, and body movements. In fact, to have any experience, neurons of the nervous system must move. But when a trauma occurs, three things happen: 1) Motion ceases; 2) memory freezes; and 3) the levels collapse. At this point, our nervous system's survival mechanism produces a generalizing response of, *"I will not let this happen again."* A scanning-searching device solidifies, which seeks out real or imagined danger to make sure it won't happen again, and a fight. flight or freeze response is evoked if it appears (often mistakenly) that it might happen again. But as you know, most of these responses are in past time, hence, they are inaccurate.

As far as collapsing the levels, when traumas are obsessively-compulsively relived, the following happens:

1. The dimensions are frozen, causing a memory picture to be formed.
2. The memory picture creates an obsessive-compulsive tendency to relive the pain but also in an attempt to *right the wrong* of this past-time situation now projected on present time, (Freud called this repetition compulsion).
3. If frozen memory is unpleasant, thus it re-enforces the False Core driver.

THE FALSE SELF

The False Self is a compensation to defend against the False Core. It acts as a buffer in the way we present ourselves to the world, i.e., our socially acceptable masks.

The False Self is an adaptive identity which becomes automatic, out of which we operate in order to survive. Unfortunately, we forget that the identity is fake, something that was made up, a creation. As the years go by, we wonder why we feel alienated and misunderstood, not realizing it is the result of being stuck in the False Core-False Self complex. Take, for example, a sexual relationship where we can't say what we need because it might be considered crude or uncool. Instead, we *pretend*. We create a fantasy and hide our true feelings in the vain hope that somehow we'll get what we want. This is the nature of the False Self—to defend against our impulses, feelings, and drives, and to buffer and hide the False Core. It forces us to *split off* from our somatic and animal selves, creating an image and hiding, our true feelings.

Recall a time when you felt angry or upset, and *put up a false front* to hide it from the world. Or a time when you felt sexually turned on and *pretended* you weren't by acting as if you were indifferent. These examples are the False Self in action.

The False Self enables us to deny or not even feel feelings, wants, or needs. The False Self is an image which we fall in love with, and try to get others to do the same. But this is unsatisfying because we know it is False, and so any love we receive can never be taken in so we have to over-do love, giving to get value, etc., etc. In this way, the False Self not only defends against the False Core but it denies our bodily sensations and animal nature.

It can't be said too often: *The False Core-False Self is not you.* This is why acting out of an assumed identity leaves you alienated, separate, misunderstood, and feeling bad. The only way to really feel unity with another is **ESSENCE** to **ESSENCE** or **I AM** to **I AM**. In order to do this, we must first discover and dismantle our False Self, our compensating identities, and our False Core driver.

THREE POINTS TO REMEMBER ABOUT THE FALSE CORE-FALSE SELF

Point 1: The first identity which is the False Core is the strongest. Let's say "I'm worthless" is the first identity. A person will continually attempt to prove his or her worth and to overcome worthlessness. But nothing can be overcome by the False Self because all attempts to prove worth are driven by worthlessness. For this reason, no matter how many times the person succeeds in life— deep down, they feel bad about themselves.

Point 2: You, the **I AM**, were there *prior* to any identities. And while the identity called "worthless" is there and after it leaves, the same **I AM** is and will be there. You cannot be your identities. Often in therapy, to get a client to appreciate that they were there prior to their identity, I say to them, "Tell me the difference between you and this image, feeling or thought called *fill in the blanks*."

Point 3: The "I" you call "you" is part of the False Core-False Self complex. When it disappears there is No "I". Nisargadatta Maharaj used to say, "Who came first, you or this 'I' (*I*-dentity)?"

Unlike other psychological schools or *spiritual* systems, Quantum Psychology does not suggest that some identities are good and others are bad. Quantum Psychology's goal is for people to find out **who they are** *prior* to their False Core-False Self not to try to heal a False concept. This is done by dismantling, the False Core-False Self and other identities so that we can become aware of **ESSENCE**, the **I AM** and beyond.

HOW TO DISMANTLE THE FALSE CORE-FALSE SELF

1. Notice the Essential Quality of **Spaciousness**.
2. Notice how it was labeled empty (as in a lack)
3. Notice the False Core-False Self and the identities that were created to defend and attempt to organize against the label and the shock of the Realization of Separation.
4. Dismantle these identities.
5. Reabsorb the identities and the observer back into **ESSENCE**.
6. Experience the Essential Qualities of your **ESSENCE**.

THE CLIFF NOTES OF
THE FALSE CORE-FALSE SELF DILEMMA

THE FALSE CORE DRIVER

The False Core Driver is the underlying conclusion, premise, concept, belief, or idea you hold about yourself which drives *all* of your psychology and all you think you are. By being brought to the light of consciousness and "on screen," we can learn to confront, investiage, question, enquire, dismantle, and go beyond it. As Nisargadatta Maharaj said, "In order to let go of something, you must first know what it is." The False Core Driver can be compared to the unconscious mind.

The False Core Driver runs on its own, like a machine on automatic. Quantum Psychology will try to help you: 1) stop the machinery; 2) enquire into its relevance; 3) dismantle it; and 4) go beyond it.

AMNESIA

Tracing your False Core requires that you see the relationship between your False Core Driver and your False Self Compensator. This normally cannot be done because there is a layer of **amnesia**, which separates the False Core from the False Self and which prevents you from knowing that they are related.

Since the False Core is so completely defended, all unwanted experiences are relegated to it. Things remain as one holographic unit unknowingly fused together by the associational trance—until the trance is broken.

Amnesia can be experienced in many different ways (as mentioned in *Trances People Live*). When this amnesia begins to dissipate, i.e., when it is gone through and beyond by realizing the relationship between the False Self to the False Core, you can "get" the entire holographic unit, get its significance, and, ultimately, go beyond it. When this relationship is not perceived, the False Core Driver and False Self Compensator are experienced as *split off* and separate from each other rather than as two sides of the same coin.

TRACING YOUR STRUCTURE

The clearer you are about the False Core Driver and its relationship to the False Self Compensator as well as the False Core defenses and distractions, the easier it will be to be to trace your entire psychology back to this one *Organizing Principle* or Structure. When you trace back to that one structure by letting go of its associations, its strength diminishes and the Essential Quality of **Spaciousness**—currently (mis)labeled emptiness (as in a lack)—dissolves, revealing the Essential Qualities of **ESSENCE**, and the stateless state or No-State State of **I AM** and the underlying unity of the **NOT-I-I**, which then move forward into your awareness.

For most people, the False Core is in the foreground and **ESSENCE** and **I AM** is in the background. When False Core-False Self is dismantled, this will be reversed and **ESSENCE** and **I AM** will become foreground and the False Core-False Self an-unnoticed background.

THE OBSERVER

The observer is part of the False core-False Self. In this way observation itself does not yield liberation because it is part of the False Core-False Self. Therefore, it could be written "Observer-False Core-False Self." To go beyond the False Core-False Self, you must also go beyond the observer of the False Core-False Self.

TRACING AND DISCOVERING YOUR FALSE CORE

Therapeutic Note:

No matter what's going on with you or your story line, if you stay with whatever you are experiencing and trace it back, you will find the False Core. The False Core is like a groove on a record, it keeps playing the same background melody over and over and over again.

The following are some examples of helping workshop participants discover their False Core.

Example #1:

Wolinsky: What is your experience?

Doris: What is my inner experience? It's disconnected.

Wolinsky:	So when you feel disconnected, what's the worst of it?
Doris:	The aloneness of it.
Wolinsky:	When you feel that loneliness of it, is that the bottom line of it? Is that the worst of it?
Doris:	It feels like being out in space without an umbilical cord.
Wolinsky:	And what would be the worst of being out in space without an umbilical cord? What's the worst of that?
Doris:	*I am nothing, I don't exist.*

Example #2:

Mike:	For me, it's like a pending death.
Wolinsky:	What's so bad about dying? What's the worst of that?
Mike:	Well, when I ask myself that, then I start to get more relaxed. Feel less distress.

Therapeutic Note:

When you acknowledge your False Core, it is so familiar you can relax into it. This is why meditation must be monitored by someone who understands that *relaxation is not the purpose of meditation* although it may be a by-product. Relaxation can come with familiarity and re-enforcement of the False Core, which is why so many seekers remain stuck. The purpose of meditation is to open up awareness of the **VOID**, **I AM** and **ESSENCE**. If meditation is done from the False Self , it reinforces the False Core.

Wolinsky:	So if you were to die, what would be the tragedy of that? What's the feeling like?
Mike:	My breathing changes. I feel a lot more relaxed.
Wolinsky:	So, if you were dead, what would that mean?
Mike:	That I would be alone and the worst of it is I wouldn't *exist*.

Therapeutic Note:

The key thing again is to stay with the experience, especially when it is painful. Follow the pain until it starts to unravel.

Mike:	But my pain always comes back.
Wolinsky:	So, what is the worst of it coming back?
Mike:	The worst of it coming back is forgetting what to do.
Wolinsky:	And if you forgot what to do, what's so bad about that?
Mike:	Then I would be in the pain.
Wolinsky:	And what's so bad about that?
Mike:	I would be *inadequate* (begins to cry).

Example #3

Lewis:	I feel powerless.
Wolinsky:	What's the worst of the powerlessness.
Lewis:	Something will happen.
Wolinsky:	What's so bad about that?
Lewis:	I would be responsible I cannot control.
Wolinsky:	And what's so bad about being out of control?
Lewis:	I would feel *inadequate or worthless*.
Wolinsky:	Why don't you sit in either one of those.

Therapeutic Note:

You can get to the False Core by following your deepest feelings. At the same time, try to see how pervasive and almost invisible the False Core is. The most important thing to find out is, what is pulling the whole chain of associations, what is at the core of it? If you get that, everything else will loosen but if you don't, things will stay the same. The False Core is called false because if you peel it back, your **ESSENTIAL CORE** emerges.

Example #4:

Ellen:	I'm wanting to really avoid this experience of like worthless, valueless, faceless, like being totally exposed. I'm not sure.
Wolinsky:	What is so bad about having no value?
Ellen:	Well, who would want to be with me?
Wolinsky:	What is so bad about no one wanting to be with you?
Ellen:	To feel this worthless and unimportant and alone.
Wolinsky:	What's so bad about feeling worthless and alone?
Ellen:	I wouldn't exist.

Wolinsky: What's so bad about non-existence?
Ellen: I would be alone. *Being alone*, that's it!
Example #5:
Ted: I feel alone.
Wolinsky: What's so bad about feeling alone?
Ted: Partly, I feel protected in that. So, it is a safe as well as a place of—I guess the worst of, I will never get out of that. I will always be like that.
Wolinsky: So you will always be isolated and alone. So what's so bad about that?
Ted: I would not have any love.
Wolinsky: Is that it'?
Ted: Yes. *I'd have no love.*

GOING BEYOND THE FALSE CORE

Step I.   Own the False Core.
Step II.   Be the False Core and observe it. Realize you look at the world through it.
Step III.   Be able to pick it up (BE IT) or put it down (UN-BE IT).
Step IV: Create it a few times and chose for it to be there.

WORKING WITH THE FALSE CORE-FALSE SELF

Knowingly, consciously and intentionally create a False Core of aloneness, unworthiness, etc., and then create some kind of over-compensation. In other words, if you are in the False Core of worthlessness, be in it and knowingly, consciously, intentionally create its compensation or False Self.

FORCE THEORY

THE FALSE CORE DRIVER

Force (Shock) → Counterforce (False Core)
False Core → (more Counterforces) False Self

In force theory, a trauma can be compared to a force coming at you. Somebody might be trying to do something to you in some way. The question after the levels are differentiated is, "What did you create in response to this force?" If you have a force coming at you, you'll then create a force to counter it. The next step is then, "What did you decide about that?" Let's take this a little further.

FORCE THEORY PROCESS

Step I.	A trauma (force) comes at you in some forceful way.
Step II.	You counter this force by creating a response to it.
Step III.	What did you decide about it?
Step IV.	What is the worst of it?
Step V	Go into the verbal **I AM** prior to the False Core.
Step VI.	Go into the non-verbal **I AM** prior to the False Core

DISMANTLING STRUCTURES, NOT RE-ENFORCING THEM

You cannot pamper I-dentities, and definitely not spiritual I-dentities. By doing this, you only strengthen the False Core's philosophy which is a defense that re-enforces the False Core driver and the False Self compensator. Which is why you can't play along with them, or flirt with them, or make your peace with them, and hope that everything will be okay—it never will. You have to confront these spiritual concepts. Yogananda Paramahansa said, "The spiritual ego is the most difficult to get rid of." And Nisargadatta Maharaj used to smash spiritual structures in order to get you free of them.

The difficulty is that there is a sense of comfort when you're in the False Core. It is a habit like smoking. Even though smoking is self-destructive, every time you smoke you feel relaxed and comfortable. The same thing with alcohol. If you like to drink, it feels great to buy a six-pack and watch TV even if it's bad for you. The False Core driver is equally familiar. That's why it is so hard to POP!

DISMANTLING THE FALSE CORE-FALSE SELF

I-DENTITIES: THE PROTOCOLS

One of the best ways to become aware of our different I-dentities is to confront them through *enquiry*, a process taught to me by Nisargadatta Maharaj. Enquiry should be considered as almost a mini-meditation.

The purpose is to ask yourself a question, notice what, if anything, *pops up* and then *acknowledge and discard it*. One should not analyze or search answers. Just notice what pops up. In this way, we can perceive what has been unknowingly pulling our attention, and free ourselves from its pull. The Indian Sage, Meher Baba, saw the ego, or the I-dentity, as an iceberg, 90 percent of which was submerged under water. Once brought into the light of awareness, the iceberg begins to melt. Quantum Psychology theorizes that the ego (False Core-False Self), is submerged (unconscious), and through enquiry it is brought to the surface, thus freeing our awareness.

Below are some general guidelines to keep in mind when you go through your enquiry. (For a more full scope, I would refer to the reader to *The Way of the Human*, Vol. II, "The False Core and the False Self.")

THE STEPS

Step I: Notice where in the I-dentity is located in your body at the present time..

Step II: Notice the I-dentity's size and shape.

Step III: Take the label off the I-dentity. Have it as energy.

Step IV: Allow the I-dentity as energy to move from the present time body to another physical location in the room, and then to become solid again.

Step V: Trace your experience back to the False Core Driver.

Step VI: Acknowledge, own, and observe the False Core.

Step VII: Un-own the False Core. This means "getting" that the False Core is not you and UN-BE the False Core.

Step VIII: Without using your thoughts, memories, emotions, associations, perceptions, attention, or intentions, Notice the non-state state of **I AM** prior to the False Core

---

QUANTUM PSYCHOLOGY PRINCIPLE:

You can never overcome or heal your False Core, you can only be free of it by realizing *it is not you.*

THE SPIRITUALIZED FALSE SELF

INTERPRETATION OF THE SHOCK OF THE REALIZATION OF SEPARATION

Spiritualization: 1) A trance whereby to avoid the pain of a person, situation, or an event, we make it "spiritual" in some way; 2) this can occur with children as they *imagine and create the fantasy* of their parents as gods or goddesses (see Wolinsky (1994) *The Dark Side of the Inner Child*).

TRANCE-PERSONAL TRANCE-FERENCE

The myth of the fall from God (i.e., the separation from God) because of a wrong action (original sin), and the concept of redemption (re-merging), are spiritualized and, ultimately, defensive metaphors which are used, in the former, to explain the shock of the Realization of Separation; and, in the latter, the imagining of re-merger with mom who is now God.

Spiritualization occurs when parents are trance-ferred onto God. This is a trance-personal trance-ference. Teachers, therapists, and gurus often implicitly—or even explicitly—offer promises of merger which trigger an age-regression in clients and seekers who then trance-fer mom and dad onto them. These promises are so powerful because they are pre-representational, infantile, and remain unquestioned to the student, client, or disciple.

They are unquestioned for two reasons: 1) they are so early that they are simply accepted as the way things are; and 2) just as it is frowned on to question Mom/Dad, so too, it is not okay to question the actions of teachers, therapists, or gurus. I knew a disciple whose guru slept with underage girls. When I told her I thought this was inappropriate, she responded by saying, "You have a lot of stuff with this teacher." "You mean if I think it's okay for a 74-year old man to sleep with 13-15 year old students, it's my stuff and my problem, not his?" She didn't answer.

To explain further, prior to the shock of the Realization of Separation, an infant holds an archaic representation of merging. When the shock of the Realization of Separation is spiritualized and mom and dad are made into gods and goddesses, years later, as an adult, you imagine they are spiritual by trying to merge with the guru mother or father (Interestingly, in Hindi, Ammaji means (dear) mother and Babaji means (dear) father). Actually you are holding onto an infantile pre-representational experience of merger, which you are now unknowingly acting out. Holding onto this re-merger with mom/God/guru is the way you resist the shock of separation.

Another way to look at it is: There is an archaic pre-representation of "you" merged with mom. You resist the shock of the Realization of Separation and hold onto the archaic representation of merger. Next, you get involved with teachers, therapists, and gurus, who become like mothers or fathers to you. The idea is to merge with them in some way, imagining that it is "spiritual." Actually, you are *acting out* the resistance to the biological and psychological shock of the Realization of Separation and calling it "spiritual."

QUANTUM PSYCHOLOGY PRINCIPLE:

The Guru/Disciple, teacher/student, and therapist/client models are, at best, an attempt to confront and heal and go beyond the shock of the Realization of Separation and stabilize in **I AM**. At its worst, they can leave people in dependent, regressive states, and in even greater pain.

SPIRITUALIZING NARCISSISM: CREATING THE PATH OR THE WAY

Notice if you have a fantasy of merging with God, guru or parent and ask yourself, Do I somehow *spiritualize* this with Gurus and God? In other words, if you follow their path, parents promise Nirvana, which, in this case, might be a house with 2.3 children. Later the spiritualized trance promises Nirvana, bliss, etc., which you might call a spiritual house with 2.3 children. The path of the Guru, the promise of enlightenment, where pain ceases and you merge with God (Mom), *can* but does not always mirror the implicit promise of merger made by parents and which, years later, has become spiritualized and justified.

SUMMARY

So again, What is the False Core? It is the one belief, concept, idea or conclusion which is identified with and which is both the organizer and driver of all your chains of thoughts, emotions, fantasies, actions, reactions and associations, etc.

For this reason it can be said, that the False Core *pulls your chain.*

And why is it called the False Core? Because it was a False assumption, from the point of view of an infant, which was (and is) based on a False conclusion. It is core because it forms the core of your psycho-emotional life.

What is the False Self? It is the False solution to the False conclusion of the False Core. It is a feeble attempt to overcome or over-compensate for this False Core conclusion.

There is, however, good news. **YOU ARE NOT YOUR FALSE CORE-FALSE SELF AND BELOW YOUR FALSE CORE-FALSE SELF LIES YOUR ESSENTIAL CORE AND THE I AM.**

7 ● ● ●

THE WAYS OF THE
FALSE CORE-FALSE SELF

In this chapter, we will describe and discuss some of the different False Core-False Selfs.

I AM IMPERFECT

FALSE CORE DRIVER:
I am imperfect. There must be something wrong with me.

FALSE SELF COMPENSATOR:
I must prove I am *not* imperfect, and that there is *not* something wrong with me. I must be perfect.

In this case, the False Core Driver, "There must be something wrong with me," "I am imperfect," like all the other False Cores, bases its entire psychology—thoughts, emotions, associations, actions, fantasies, dreams, wishes, desires, etc.—on a false premise and conclusion. Since this premise arises and is solidified quite early in life and resisted due to its association and fusion with the shock of the Realization of Separation, the False Core of "There must be something wrong with me," "I am imperfect" formulates that the way to Nirvana is by merging with mom. Later, if psychologized, the way to re-merger is seen as getting healthy and getting what you want. If it is *spiritualized*, the process is seen as becoming enlightened; if *relationship-ized*, merger is seen as being accomplished by finding the *perfect* relationship; and if *workized*, merger is attempted to be found through perfection at work. This solution is falsely imagined to be accomplished through the False Self Compensator trying to prove that there is nothing wrong with me and/or that I am perfect.

The problem is that the first formulated conclusion—in this case "There must be something wrong with me," "I am imperfect"—is the strongest and organizes and rules this closed loop. Subjectively speaking, there is no way out. Why? Because this False Core premise always proves itself. In other words, it will always subjectively prove that *I am imperfect, there must be something wrong with me.*

Since the shock of the Realization of Separation and its accompanying premise that "I am imperfect," "There must be something wrong with me," is resisted, an obsessive compulsive tendency emerges. As with all tendencies, which exhibit *repetition-compulsion*, the underlying belief is, "If I can just do it again, maybe I can do it right and the outcome will be different. Thus, the False Core "I am imperfect," "There must be something wrong with me" is re-enacted, re-sisted, and re-created as a repetition compulsion— acted out again and again in the hope of having a better or even *perfect* outcome. In this way, some "New" therapies use the False Self in an attempt to create a different or *perfect* outcome. Ultimately, however, it only re-enforces the False Core. To counter this premise, the major formulation of the False Self Compensator is, "I have to be perfect or prove I am not imperfect or defective," or "If only things were perfect, Nirvana—or merger with mom, later generalized to the world, God, etc.—would occur."

It's possible that "therapies" which recreate the trauma and place a happy, perfect, or desired ending on the past story or memory add insight to the problem. But in the final analysis, it is the False Self which places the perfect ending on the memory in its attempt to overcome the False Core, thus re-enforcing it. This ultimately re-enforces the memory by using the False Self Compensator and its *repetition-compulsion*, which doesn't take into account that the story was created by the nervous system and comes neurologically after the fact to justify itself. I am not trying to put down any form of therapy. Instead, I am proposing that if our intention is to find out **WHO WE ARE**, then psycho-spiritual systems need to be looked at to see if they're helping in the endeavor.

From this point on we will write *Identity* as *I-dentity* to denote it as an "I", which at this level, is a construction of the nervous system since it arises later than the original experience. The construction of an I-dentity is used to organize, justify, and give a reason for the unwanted experience, behavior, or action.

EXPERIENTIAL CONCLUSION
(ASK YOURSELF OR HAVE ANOTHER PERSON GUIDE YOU)

1. Without using your thoughts, memory, emotions, associations, perceptions, attention, or intentions, is there something wrong with you, nothing wrong with you or neither?

2. Without using your thoughts, memory, emotions, associations, perceptions, attention, or intentions, are you perfect, imperfect or neither?

3. Without using your thoughts, memory, emotions, associations perceptions, attention, or intentions, what does perfection or imperfection even mean?

4. Without using your thoughts, memory, emotions, associations perceptions, attention, or intentions, what is emptiness?

Notice the Stateless state or No-State state, the Non-verbal **I AM** *prior* to thoughts, memory, emotions, associations, perceptions, attention or intentions.

I AM WORTHLESS

FALSE CORE DRIVER:

I am worthless, I have no value.

FALSE SELF COMPENSATOR:

I must prove I am not worthless and that I have value.

This False Core Driver, too, with the premise of "I am worthless," "I have no value," describes a conclusion which *theoreti-*

THE BEGINNER'S GUIDE •••

cally began to solidify between the age of 5-12 months. I use the word *theoretically* because it is basically unprovable.

Now, the False Core of "I am worthless," "I have no value," uses the False Self of "I have to prove that I am worthy," or that "I have value." If this strategy fails, the person with this False Core would be left with "I am worthless," "I have no value." Attempts to overcome this worthless I-dentity are: Becoming an over-giver, making others dependent on them, telling themselves or others how great, beautiful or professionally gifted and successful they are to get flattery and hence feel valuable. In this way they try to create an image of worth, wealth, and value. All of these, of course, are merely attempts to hide the internal state of worthlessness and no value, and to get others to flatter them so that they can feel like they have value.

The False Core Driver and the False Self Compensator are holographic. Each is inseparable from the other, like two sides of a coin. All False Core drivers contain within them a self-fulfilling prophesy, namely, they prove themselves.

To recap: The False Core of "I am worthless," "I have no value," has as its goal, "If only I can become worthy and have value, by whatever means, I will be able to merge with Mom, i.e., reach Nirvana, and we can be one again." But this can never happen. For, as with all False Core-False Selves, the *obsessive-compulsive* tendency to right the wrong by acting it out through repetition compulsion is not in present time and only serves to re-play the same old story or song, thus, re-enforcing the False Core again and again. It is like playing a record, in this case, the music is always the same, it is just the words (present time events) which appear to change.

EXPERIENTIAL CONCLUSION

(ASK YOURSELF OR HAVE ANOTHER PERSON GUIDE YOU)

1. Without using your thoughts, memory, emotions, associations, perceptions, attention, or intentions, are you worthless, worthy valuable, valueless or neither?

2. Without using your thoughts, memory, emotions, associations, perceptions, attention, or intentions, what does worthy, worthless, value or valueless even mean?

3. Without using your thoughts, memory, emotions, associations, perceptions, attention, or intentions, what does empty or emptiness even mean?

Notice the Stateless state or No-State state, the Non-verbal **I AM** *prior* to thoughts, memory, emotions, associations, perceptions, attention or intentions.

Since the False Core Conclusion is fused with the shock of the Realization of Separation, it is part of the nervous system's survival mechanism.

The shock and the "I am worthless," or any False Core for that matter, must not, under any circumstances, happen again— hence the False Self solution.

Stephen H. Wolsinsky

I CAN NOT DO

FALSE CORE DRIVER:

I cannot do, decide or act

FALSE SELF COMPENSATOR:

I have to prove I can do, decide or act by becoming an over-achiever or an over-doer.

The False Core of "I cannot do," "I have an inability to do," and "I do not do" are widely used and defended, especially in Western culture. I have a dear friend who has the largest Institute in the world in the area of her specialty. But she always feels as though she does not "do." To overcompensate, she has become an over-doer. Though over-achievers are highly valued in our culture, still my friend can find no meaningful solutions to her problems. This is because she is part of a closed system into which no feedback penetrates, hence she is at the mercy of her False Core-False Self.

There is a real subjective unconscious and unacknowledged feeling of impotence and sometimes even paralysis. This False Core of "inability to do," of "I cannot do," is seemingly based on other facts; but actually is an unconscious and subjective experience.

This particular False Self Compensator tries to handle its subjective experience not doing with vanity, which we define as looking outside yourself through another's eyes, to see how you are doing. In this way, you perform—unknowingly for your parents later generalized to others—and see yourself through the eyes of another to make sure you're doing enough or doing it right. Vanity is a way of not being in present time experience, in other words, I am outside of myself seeing how you see me. An example would be dressing not for comfort but so that people will think I'm rich or chic. In this way, you are neither in your body nor even aware of it. I once knew a woman who complained about back pain yet continued to wear five-inch high heels. I mentioned to her how bad that was for her back and she said, "I like the look."

This False Self Compensator also uses self-deceit which causes individuals to exaggerate their abilities. If they lean toward the False Self Compensator side, they tend to exaggerate and become grandiose about their ability *to do* anything. If they are more fused with the False Core, they are more enmeshed in self-deception, and fooling themselves about what they have done. A business-woman who once saw me for therapy used to say, "I can make it happen. I work twenty-four hours a day." She not only exaggerated her ability *to do* but also her so-called working hours. She was more on the False Self Compensator side. Her self-deceit was exaggerating her achievements and her ability to do, which is the opposite of the earlier situation of *I cannot do.*

I once saw a man in therapy who had a relationship outside of his marriage which had been going on for years. When his wife found out, she was extremely upset. But when he told me about it, the man said, "I didn't *do* anything." This is the extraordinary self deception of the False Core-False Self complex.

EXPERIENTIAL CONCLUSION
(ASK YOURSELF OR HAVE ANOTHER PERSON GUIDE YOU)

1. Without using your thoughts, memory, emotions, associations, perceptions, attention, or intentions, are you a doer a not doer or neither?

2. Without using your thoughts, memory, emotions, associations, perceptions, attention, or intentions, what does doing or not doing even mean?

3. Without using your thoughts, memory, emotions, associations or perceptions what does empty mean.

Notice the Stateless state or No-State state, the Non-verbal **I AM** *prior* to thoughts, memory, emotions, associations, perceptions, attention or intentions.

I AM INADEQUATE
FALSE CORE DRIVER:
I am inadequate.

FALSE SELF COMPENSATOR:
I must prove that I am not inadequate, that I am adequate and smart.

The False conclusion of this False Core Driver is "I am inadequate." As with all the other False Core drivers, "I am Inadequate" drives the machine of its psychology and associations. In review, a False Core Drives the False Self Compensator to obsessively-compulsively fantasize reaching Nirvana (merger with mom, later psychologized as "health" or spiritualized as God) through becoming or proving adequacy. This tendency of the False Self is weaker than that of the False Core because:

1) The False Core driver is the first conclusion and, therefore, organizes and drives the False Self solution like a machine. In short, no False Core Driver—no False Self Compensator.

2) The False Core-False Self is holographic and it is a closed loop.

3) The False Core ultimately leaves each False Self Compensator exacerbated and frustrated because you can never overcome, heal or transform through over-compensation because the solution must be false since it is based on a false conclusion, and a *False Cause*. (The effect of the observer as part of the False Core-False Self complex will be discussed later.)

The problem with the False Core-False Self-Observer complex is that psychological and spiritual attempts to heal, transform, convert vices (sins) to virtues, move from unhealthy to healthy, disintegrative to integrative, reframe, reassociate, re-decide, get rid of, go beyond, surrender, overcome, etc., etc., etc.—all of these are the work of the False Self Compensator and, hence, they only re-enforce the False Core.

The False Core driver is simply a False conclusion, a False premise, a False assumption, and a *False Cause*. The False Core driver is misinformation about oneself and must be discarded. The False Self compensator is thus doomed to fail because it is a solution based on a false conclusion.

The False Core is a concept which grew out of a 5 to 12 month old infant's mind. It is not something that needs to be healed, transformed, or made better, etc. Conversely, in Quantum Psychology, the way out of this dilemma is by taking the way in:

1. Being aware of your False Core driver.
2. Observing your False Core.
3. Being willing to feel the pain of your False Core driver.
4. Tracing the chains of associations and behavior back from the False Self Compensator to the False Core driver, thus breaking the linkage which binds them and "you".

5. Tracing it back to the verbal **I AM.**

6. Going into the non-verbal **I AM** (no thoughts, memory, emotions, associations or perceptions, *prior* to the False Core Driver and its verbal formulations and representations.

7. Dismantling your False Core Driver and False Self Compensator.

PSYCHO-SPIRITUAL DEFENSES
(NOT LIMITED TO THE FALSE CORE-FALSE SELF)

1) Proving adequacy through the psychological defense of being over-analytic to avoid the False Core Driver.

2) Pathologizing: An action of the False Self of projecting a psychological pathology onto another, so that you feel less inadequate, and worthless.

Hypervigilance, the psychological component of the biological searching-seeking mechanism, is rooted in the nervous system's fight/flight, overgeneralizing mechanism. This process is not actually in present time since it was organized by the child to handle the outer chaos of mom/dad/society, etc. This age-regressed tendency is an attempt to organize (mis)perceived chaos in present time, and as such it runs on automatic. Hence, its over-analyzing and over-categorizing mechanisms re-enforces this age-regressed tendency.

EXTREMELY IMPORTANT

As with all False Core Drivers, reasons and causes are falsely attributed to events as to why I feel *fill in the blank*, to justify feelings and to offer a way out. In this way it must be understood that you (the nervous system) has come up with a *false* reason, a *False Cause*, to explain why the separation occurred. The *False* conclusion is the False Core and it is solidified in theory at age 5-12 months. It is a false and inaccurate assessment of the natural process of separation. The first False conclusion assumes that if only I were not *fill in the blank*, or if only I were *fill in the blank*, the inevitable separation would not have occurred.

What you are doing is trying to solve the problem of separation by imagining a reason and attributing a cause as to why it happened. But your conclusions and causes are False, as to why you are separate. The False conclusion is an attempt to give a reason and cause for the inevitable separation. The *False Self Compensator must therefore be a False solution since it is based on a False conclusion.* In this way the False solution is erroneous and false because it is based on a false and erroneous conclusion drawn by an infant from the shock of the Realization of Separation.

AN ESSENTIAL COMPARISON

All False Core Drivers experience some lack because unknowingly they are comparing themselves to **ESSENCE**. In other words, "I'm imperfect," "I'm worthless," "I'm unable to do," "I'm inadequate" are all unknowingly being compared to **ESSENCE** .

It should be further noted that a lack can never be handled at a psychological level because the I-dentity at first *appears* to be facing outward toward the world. It judges itself against others, comes up short, and feels inadequate. In reality, the I-dentities are facing inward, comparing themselves to **ESSENCE**. The truth is that I-dentities are less than—or have a lack compared to—**ESSENCE**. For this reason, the way to handle the lack is to dismantle I-dentities and then reabsorb the False Core Driver and False Self Compensator I-dentities back into **ESSENCE**—and then experience **THE ESSENTIAL QUALITIES OF ESSENCE.**

EXPERIENTIAL CONCLUSION

(ASK YOURSELF OR HAVE ANOTHER PERSON GUIDE YOU)

1. Without using your thoughts, memory, emotions, associations, perceptions, attention, or intentions, are you adequate, inadequate or neither?

2. Without using your thoughts, memory, emotions, associations, perceptions, attention, or itentions, what does adequate or inadequate mean?

3. Without using your thoughts, memory, emotions, associations, perceptions, attention, or intentions, what does empty mean

Notice the Stateless state or No-State state of the Non-verbal **I AM** *prior* to thoughts, memory, emotions, associations, perceptions, attention or intentions.

THE BEGINNER'S GUIDE •••

I DO NOT EXIST

FALSE CORE DRIVER:

I don't exist, I am nothing, I have nothing.

FALSE SELF COMPENSATOR:

I must prove that I exist, that I am something, that I have something.

The False Core Driver of "I do not exist" is one of the most interesting and, in Quantum Psychology workshops, the most frequent. I have found this False Core-False Self to frequently appear in ashrams, meditation groups, therapy groups, and spiritual groups. From a Quantum Psychology perspective, there are two basic reasons for this:

First, in many Eastern spiritual groups the philosophy of no-self, observe and watch, re-enforce the *most primal defense of this False Core Driver which is over-observation.*

Second, according to Reich and Lowen, this False Core Driver can be likened to the definition of schizoid in "character analysis," which is developed in utero. This means that this False Core occurs not only at an energetic-genetic level, but it can also be seen within the bony structure of an individual. From a Quantum Psychology perspective, this means that this False Core begins to solidify not at 5-12 months but in utero.

Because of such early development, its obsessive-compulsive nature is even more deeply embedded in the body than any of the other False Core-False Selves. Thus, the underlying, non-verbal, pre-representational structure of "I do not exist" dwells far outside of awareness. This might explain its predominance in meditation groups which search for answers in Eastern philosophy and religion. At the same time, it is important to differentiate this False Core Driver from the no-self of the East. In the East there is no self because **THERE IS ONLY ONE SUBSTANCE.** In this way it is true at the level of the **VOID OF UNDIFFERENTIATED CONSCIOUSNESS.** At the level of bio-psychology, no-self or non-existence is untrue, and painful.

However, because it can be confused with the Eastern no-self, it is easy for the False Core Driver of "I do not exist" to confuse levels and choose a Buddhist (no-self) or Advaita (non-duality), a no-I approach which only re-enforces the False Core Driver of "I do not exist."

In the view of Quantum Psychology, teachers or gurus who allow students to stay around and do a practice which re-enforces their False Core is like offering an alcoholic another drink. This also suggests that the thinking, cognitive and analytic therapies as well as those which support self observation, often re-enforce the over-thinking distraction and defensive over-observation of this False Core of "I do not exist."

Quantum Psychology asks therapists and spiritual teachers to discern who is in front of them, and not re-enforce the False Core. When necessary, we recommend referring out regardless of any economic loss. It is my understanding that originally teachers in the Sufi tradition sent students where they needed to go. But sometimes teachers don't see the shortcomings of their own systems. Possibly this is because an "I don't exist" teacher has his or her own schizoid structure, insight barrier or intellectual armoring. In this way, they hold onto students when the system is inappropriate for them, through the re-enforcement of the Observer-False Core Driver-False Self Compensator, not perceiving their system's limitations or their own personal shortcomings.

The distractor I-dentities of the False Core Driver "I don't exist" are "I don't know" and "I have to know." The False Core Driver of "I don't exist," however, accumulates information because it imagines it is nothing and has nothing. If I have "something" (i.e., information and ideas), "I exist." For this reason there is an obsessive-compulsive addiction to knowing and accumulating information to avoid the pain of non-existence.

CONCLUSION

The distractor inner states consist of, I feel nothing, over-thinking, a projected "they" might engulf me, withdrawal into spiritualized defensive silence. The spiritual defense is over-observing, I am nothing, there is no self, there is no-I. As with all False Cores:

1. Trace it.
2. Notice it.
3. Experience it.
4. Without believing it, peel it back to your False Core ("I don't exist").

5. Experience this.
6. Be in the verbal **I AM**.
7. Then be in the non-verbal **I AM** prior to the False Core Driver, with no thoughts, memory, emotions, associations or perceptions.

EXPERIENTIAL CONCLUSION
(ASK YOURSELF OR HAVE ANOTHER PERSON GUIDE YOU)

1. Without using your thoughts, memory, emotions, associations, perceptions, attention, or intentions, do you exist, not exist, or neither?

2. Without using your thoughts, memory, emotions, associations, perceptions, attention, or intentions, what does existence or non-existence even mean?

3. Without using your thoughts, memory, emotions, associations, perceptions, attention, or intentions, what does empty mean?

Notice the Stateless state or No-State state of the Non-verbal **I AM** *prior* to thoughts, memory, emotions, associations, perceptions, attention or intentions.

I AM ALONE

FALSE CORE DRIVER:
I am alone.

FALSE SELF COMPENSATOR:
I must not be alone, I must connect. The over-connector.

This False Core Driver has the conclusion "I am alone." As with all the others, this False Core will adapt spiritual and psychological philosophies to try to compensate for, or justify, the virtues of being alone—for instance, that it's more spiritual. The greatest fear of this False Core, more than being alone, is to be shunned. The False Self Compensator, on the other hand, has an obsessive-compulsive tendency to "over connect" as a way to overcome the "I am alone." As with each False Core-False Self, staying with the "I am alone," is more honest although more painful and de-compensated than staying with the False Self, in this case, the obsessive-compulsive, "I have to connect."

At the time of connection, though there is a high and a relief from "I am alone"; however, like a drug addict, the False Self Compensator needs more and more compensation to get the same relief. Furthermore, the compensation can often become so integrated, as in a lifestyle, that the person thinks, "That's the way I am."

Many spiritual, psychological practices, or techniques can be also used to make a connection, and during moments of relaxation and/or insight, there is a relief from the False Core. But as soon as the practice ceases, the pain springs back. Spiritual and Psychological disciplines are often unaware of the False Core-False Self, and are unable to handle the underlying pain and unknowingly re-enforce the over-connecting. To alleviate the suffering, spiritual teachers might suggest *more* mantra, yantra, or tantra. Or in the case of psychology, more communication, more feeling your feelings, and in short, more connecting. Of course, this feels natural; but as my psychology mentor, Dr. Eric Marcus once said, "When someone says, 'Well, this is just how I am', they are acknowledging their *characterological structure*." In other words, not questioning but *assuming* this was how they are. These types of techniques oftentimes re-enforce the False Core since it is the False Self Compensator doing the spiritual or psychological practice, namely, seeking Nirvana through connection.

> QUANTUM PSYCHOLOGY PRINCIPLE:
>
> Psychological and Spiritual disciplines are often undertaken by the False Self Compensator to overcome the False Core. This is why it's impossible to stabilize or go beyond pain because the False Self and the False Core are one unit.

EXPERIENTIAL CONCLUSION
(ASK YOURSELF OR HAVE ANOTHER PERSON GUIDE YOU)

1. Without using your thoughts, memory, emotions, associations, perceptions, attention, or intentions, are you alone, connected or neither?

2. Without using your thoughts, memory, emotions, associations, perceptions, attention, or intentions, what does alone, connected or shunned even mean?

3. Without using your thoughts, memory, emotions, associations, perceptions, attention, or intentions, what does empty mean?

Notice the Stateless state or No-State state of the Non-verbal **I AM** *prior* to thoughts, memory, emotions, associations, perceptions, attention or intentions.

I AM INCOMPLETE

FALSE CORE DRIVER:

I am incomplete, There must be something missing, I am not enough.

FALSE SELF COMPENSATOR:

I must get whole, complete, completed or full through experiences.

THE SPIRITUAL DEFENSE OF THE FALSE SELF

The False Self uses spiritual defenses and spirituality to seek blissful *heart* experiences as a way to defend and reframe pain into lessons, solutions, motivations or opportunities to justify or overcome the pain of the False Core. But the fulfillment which this False Self seeks can never be found in spiritual teachers, spiritual or psychological re-frames. Because this False Core is unable to deal with its imagined incompleteness, this False Self runs from teacher to teacher and from psychology to psychology, gathering spiritual and psychological experiences without ever going deeply into anything. I've known many people with this False Core-False Self who distracted themselves and lived by the super-standards and rules of a rigid spiritual or psychological ideal discipline *as if* this would bring them closer to God, (Mom), and keep them from "I am Incomplete."

The False Core "I am incomplete" or "There must be some thing missing" seeks their imagined Nirvana through enjoyable experiences; hence, they become over-experiencers. The deep incompleteness of this False Core yields an obsessive-compulsive tendency to seek pleasurable experiences to fill in what is missing, or where they feel not enough. They feel "If only I could have more, get more, find out what you've got and get it, I could fill in the missing pieces and feel complete." "If the missing piece within me were filled I would be able to reach Nirvana, enlightenment, and, unconsiously, oneness with mom."

Another problem facing this False Core-False Self is that what goes up must come down. In other words, no matter how high they fly, people always find themselves back in their False Core. Actually, there is a major dissociation between the pain of this False Core and the fake optimistic, pretend happy False Self. This is because the False Self knows nothing of the pain of incompleteness which is driving its pleasure seeking. A layer of amnesia separates the False Core from the False Self, a layer which, in its depth and strength, is a powerful deterrent against knowing or experiencing the False Core of "I am incomplete."

This False Self looks for pleasure to feel complete, not knowing, it is on a treadmill. If the treadmill stops, even for a moment, they must find yet another positive, pleasurable experience to overcome the incomplete one. It is extremely difficult for them to get in touch with their pain or allow another person to have their pain. They are driven to constantly see the bright side, or to build people up so that they can bring them down as a way to avoid and distract themselves from their own incompleteness which they fear will overwhelm them.

EXPERIENTIAL CONCLUSION
(ASK YOURSELF OR HAVE ANOTHER PERSON GUIDE YOU)

1. Without using your thoughts, memory, emotions, associations, perceptions, attention, or intentions, are you complete, incomplete or neither?

2. Without using your thoughts, memory, emotions, associations, perceptions, attention, or intentions, what does complete or incomplete even mean?

3. Without using your thoughts, memory, emotions, associations, perceptions, attention, or intentions, what does empty mean?

Notice the Stateless state or No-State state of the Non-verbal **I AM** *prior* to thoughts, memory, emotions, associations, perceptions, attention or intentions.

I AM POWERLESS

FALSE CORE DRIVER:

I am powerless.

FALSE SELF COMPENSATOR:

I must prove I am not powerless by acting as if I were powerful.

This False Core-False Self has the obsessive compulsive tendency to seek power and to resist powerlessness. Developmental psychology suggests that the infant sees mom as all powerful and magical. In this way, the infant attempts to fuse with mommy's imagined magical powers of omniscience, omnipotence, and omnipresence. This can be seen in the *outward behavior* of religious leaders, politicians and those whose general motivating principle *appears* to be power. For the infant this is, "I will enter Nirvana, that is, merge with mom, if I am not powerless but powerful."

It should be remembered that it is very difficult to determine another's False Core Driver. But it is easy to determine the False Self Compensator by observing outward behavior.

FALSE POWER

Real power comes from within. There is no question that miracles occur, but you have to realize that *it's not personal.* There is no question that gurus who know **THAT** might have powers; but if they are truthful, they will admit that they are not the source of that power, nor do they allow others to see them that way. They are amazed, astonished, and surprised by what occurs or can occur around them. But sometimes gurus, therapists, and teachers get hooked into the adulation they receive, because of their uncooked seeds of feeling powerless.

EXPERIENTIAL CONCLUSION
(ASK YOURSELF OR HAVE ANOTHER PERSON GUIDE YOU)

1. Without using your thoughts, memory, emotion, associations, perceptions, attention, or intentions, are you powerless, powerful or neither?

2. Without using your thoughts, memory, emotion, associations, perceptions, attention, or intentions, what does powerful or powerless even mean?

3. Without using your thoughts, memory, emotion, associations, perceptions, attention, or intentions, what does empty mean?

Notice the Stateless state or No-State state of the Non-verbal **I AM** *prior* to thoughts, memory, emotions, associations, perceptions, attention or intentions.

I AM LOVELESS

FALSE CORE DRIVER:
I am loveless; There is no love.

FALSE SELF COMPENSATOR:
I must prove I am not loveless. I must be lovable and loving.

The False Core Driver of "I am loveless, there is no love" compensates with a facade of loving and acceptance of what's happening. But underneath this mask is a passive, sometimes aggressive, persona encased in a coat of armor. This is the result of on-going spiritualization and the denial of "I am loveless, there is no love."

In this case, the False Self Compensator acts overly caring and seeks love and spirituality. But they can never make up in present time for the love which they did not get or concluded that they did not get, which was the reason for the separation from mom. As with all False Cores, they never get what they want and always wind up feeling loveless or whatever their False Core is. This leads to passive-aggressive anger as the rage around separation is generalized to the world. This anger can never come out directly, though, because of the overriding fear that the consequence will mean that

69

others will withdraw their love. This propels this False Self into more over-giving False love to overcompensate even more in this never-ending cycle. Another way to look at it is: Merging with Mom equals love, separation equals no love. Therefore, separation must be avoided and resisted at all costs. To express anger or confront anything directly could mean No love which would trigger the memory of the dreaded shock of separation.

EXPERIENTIAL CONCLUSION
(ASK YOURSELF OR HAVE ANOTHER PERSON GUIDE YOU)

1. Without using your thoughts, emotions, memory, associations, perceptions, attention, or intentions, is there no-love, love or neither?

2. Without using your thoughts, emotions, memory, associations or perceptions are you lovable, unlovable or neither.

3. Without using your thoughts, emotions, memory, associations, perceptions, attention, or intentions, what is love?

4. Without using your thoughts, emotions, memory, associations, perceptions, attention, or intentions, what does empty mean?

Notice the Stateless state or No-State state of the Non-verbal I AM *prior* to thoughts, memory, emotions, associations, perceptions, attention or intentions.

SECTION TWO •••

THE DIMENSIONS OF MANIFESTATION IN DEPTH

8 ●●●

THE FIRST DIMENSION
OF AWARENESS

THE EXTERNAL DIMENSION

THE FIRST DIMENSION: THE EXTERNAL DIMENSION

This is the first dimension. There's the external world, there's my house, my room, I'm talking to you on the telephone. There are all the objects and people in my life, and all the rules of the external dimension. If I rob a bank and get caught, I'll probably go to jail. At first this dimension seems easy because, of course, there is a person, there is a car, there is a bank, etc. Still, all of our internal dialogues, trances, False Core-False Self, etc., really stop us from fully realizing and experiencing the present time external as the present time external. What is true at the external level *may not be true* at any other level.

THE EXTERNAL CONTEXT RULES

Different contexts or external circumstances pull up different internal responses, especially unresolved issues. To illustrate, imagine everything is going well in your life. You are not in a relationship, but work, friends, lifestyle—all are fine and you are feeling good about yourself. Soon you meet someone and it gets sexual.

All of a sudden your psychological and emotional issues come up. Why? *Different externals* pull up *different unresolved internals.*

EXERCISES FOR THE EXTERNAL DIMENSION

THE EXTERNAL WORLD

Step 1.   Slowly look around the room at people and objects. Notice the memories, internal voices, and associations which automatically pop up for you.

Step 2.   Now without using your thoughts, memory, emotions, associations, perceptions, attention, or intentions, look around the room.

Step 3.   Notice the difference between Step 1 and Step 2.

EXERCISE: STABILIZING AWARENESS

The object of this exercise is to look at an object in the room and then withdraw your energy from it, thus, eliminating the knowledge or information of the object along with the thought or impression. (Vijnana Bhairava; Singh)

Step 1.   First, pick out something in the room. Now, pull back your attention. In other words, your attention is moving forward, going out toward a particular object, like the couch, for instance. Well, instead of going forward, pull your attention back. As you look at the object, pull your attention back, *prior* to having the impression of the object.

Step 2.   Let your eyes close for a second, then open them and make eye contact with a person. Let your attention withdraw, *prior* to any knowledge, information, impressions, or thoughts you have about that person. Turn your attention backward, drawing it backward.

Step 3.   Next, close your eyes again. Open them and make eye contact with another person, and again gently withdraw your attention *prior* to

any thoughts, impressions or information you
have about that person.

CONCLUSION

Notice how different the experience of the external world
and people are without thoughts or impressions, etc. This is the
external as the external, and experiencing it as it is, is what Suzuki
Roshi called *beginner's mind*, a mind where the external just is,
without our judgments, evaluations, or significancees about it.

9 ●●●

THE THINKING DIMENSION

THE SECOND DIMENSION

THE THINKING DIMENSION

The Thinking Dimension contains not only thoughts, beliefs, values but also images, fantasies, memories, associations, and concepts, etc. What is true at the Thinking Dimension may not be true at any other dimension.

UNCOOKED SEEDS REVISITED

We all know what uncooked seeds are by now. Well, in Quantum Psychology, you will learn to process the uncooked seeds of your psychology in the frying pan of awareness so that they can no longer sprout and bear their poisonous fruit.

Any uncooked seed which remains unacknowledged has the potential to sprout as soon as the context (external dimension) changes, or as soon as you move from one external dimension to another.

Quantum Psychology suggests becoming aware of what is going on and dismantling your False Core-False Self, which, although primarily at the thinking, emotional, and biological level, is triggered by variations in the external. In this way, your uncooked seeds no longer sprout, so that your awareness is no longer grabbed and pulled out of **ESSENCE, I AM, NOT-I-I**, etc.

And the Number One uncooked seed of your psychology is the False Core-False Self because it drives the entire machinery of what you call *you*.

QUANTUM PSYCHOLOGY EXERCISE

To get a sense of thoughts as things that come and go, very gently let your eyes close as you sit or lie comfortably. Each time thought crosses your mind, notice it and ask yourself, "Where does this thought subside to?"

As you notice the activity in your mind, it appears at first as a pattern of thoughts . . . thoughts . . . thoughts. But as you pursue this exercise, soon you realize the space between two thoughts. When you do, *stay* in the space between two thoughts.

EXERCISE

Step I: Notice a thought or feeling you are having.
Step II: Withdraw your attention from the thought or feeling prior to any knowledge or information about it.
Step III: View the thought or emotion from that space.
Step IV: Notice what happens.

CULTIVATING THE SECOND DIMENSIONAL AWARENESS

ASPECTS OF CONSCIOUSNESS

(This process was originally written about in *Trances People Live—Healing Approaches in Quantum Psychology* (1986).)

Differentiated consciousness involves the making of distinctions. It is that subtle something which marks differences. Differentiated consciousness lets us know the difference between a table and a chair, your arm and my head. (Please note that differentiated consciousness possesses a separate "I" which has all the psychological aspects of preferences, comparisons, etc. **UNDIFFEREN-TIATED CONSCIOUSNESS** does not have or know preferences or comparison. **UNDIFFERENTIATED CONSCIOUSNESS** is **VOID**er than the **VOID** itself and has no separate "I". Hence, the Zen patriarch said, "The great way is easy, except for those who have preferences."

On a more subtle level, it lets us know the difference between a thought and a feeling, a sound and an vision, a past memory, and present time. Unfortunately, however, consciousness frequently muddles these distinctions, which causes chaos as to what is occurring in the present time, and what has occurred in the past.

Before we can appreciate the **VOID OF UNDIFFERENTIATED CONSCIOUSNESS**, it might be helpful to distinguish the different aspects of consciousness and what they are. I discussed this approach in relation to trances in *Trances People Live* (1986) and *The Dark Side of the Inner Child* (1993). As I mentioned earlier, Nisargadatta Maharaj once said, "In order to give something up, you must first know what it is."

Our first step in this process is to *identify and define* the aspects of consciousness which often act as trances so that we can begin to get clear about the meaning of the words and notice how they take us out of present-time reality.

DEFINITIONS

The following definitions were all drawn from *The American College Dictionary*. (1963).

THOUGHT: The single act of thinking; an idea or a notion.

INTERNAL DIALOGUE: Also referred to in *Trances People Live* as a post-hypnotic suggestion. These are internal voices which suggest certain outcomes. For example, the internal voice, "It will never work out," or "I know you're going to break up with me so I'll detach and not get involved."

INTUITION: A direct understanding independent of any reasoning process. An immediate cognition of an object not inferred or determined previously.

Therapeutic Note

I want to give an example of intuition since it's often confused with training. Let's say someone comes to me for therapy and says, "I have a problem with relationships." If I say, "I wonder if this has something to do with your parents," this is not intuition, it's training. If I say to the client, "Did you have a dog named Fred who died when you were two?" and he says, "Yeah!" that's intuition. To paraphrase Pir Vilayat, a Sufi teacher, intuition exists when there was no way you could have known. Training, on the other hand, is what you have been taught to know or do.

MEMORY: The mental capacity or faculty of retaining and reviving impressions, or of recalling or recognizing previous experiences.

BLOCKING OUT: The act of not seeing or remembering an event or situation.

REACTION: Action in response to some influence or event; the action caused by the resistance to another action.

DISSOCIATION: Dissociation is spacing-out, going on automatic pilot or disappearing.

CONFUSION: The act of creating a state of not knowing. Generally, this is caused by not knowing what to do or resisting a present-time occurrence.

FANTASY: A created dream, also called hypnotic dreaming, which is often used to buffer oneself against present-time pain. For example, feeling lonely and depressed and fantasizing someone will come and take you away from all of this.

HALLUCINATION: Existing in imagination or fancy, appearance of mental images. This is when old images like Mom or Dad pop into your awareness without your control.

BELIEF: A solidified thought which can become a value or evaluation of self or the world. It can be attitudinal if it determines a way of life or living.

OBSERVATION: The act of observing a thought, emotion, association, sensation, person, etc. It is part of the thought association itself although it appears as separate. It might appear to always be there or be prior to the thought, etc., when it actually arises with it, and some even believe the observer created it. It is important to note that often observation contains judgment (this is good or bad), evaluation (this means this or that), and significance (this is more important than that).

WITNESSING: The act of noticing or perceiving (without judgment, evaluation or significance). Beyond the observer-observed dyad.

Therapeutic Note

It is extremely important to note that, ultimately, the ob-server must fall away in order to stabilize in **ESSENCE I AM, NOT-I-I**, etc. *The observer is part of the personality and the mind* (to be discussed later). To explain further, Quantum Psychology states that "Anything you know about cannot be you." Why? Because each knowing belongs to a separate knower, and you are beyond the knower or the known. Therefore, since you can be aware of the observer—you are not the observer. The observer can have a disso-ciative tendency. Often the observer can be used to rein-force defenses against unwanted feelings or other dimen-sions, especially emotional and biological (to be discussed later). As mentioned earlier in Quantum Consciousness, we must be free to merge with and either *be* something or *not be* something. If we are not free to BE it, and NOT BE it, we are not free. This is *Quantum Observation*, which is different from just observing.

CONDENSATION: A condensed state or form, the act of con-densing or shrinking down; the act of reducing a gas or vapor to a liquid or solid form. Condensations are everything. Since "Every-thing is made of emptiness and form is condensed emptiness," then all of the above are condensations of **THAT ONE CONSCIOUS-NESS** (See Wolinsky,1993, *Quantum Consciousness: The Guide to Experiencing Quantum Psychology*).

Therapeutic Note

This is extremely important to understand. Einstein has said that "Everything is emptiness and form is condensed emptiness." In this way, you can begin to see all manifes-tations as condensed **EMPTINESS**—including the ob-server-knower of thoughts, emotions, and objects. This is a step in moving from the observer-observed knower-known dyad into the **NOT-I-I** of pure awareness or **WIT-NESSING** .

WORKING WITH THE ASPECTS OF CONSCIOUSNESS
EXERCISE: USING THE MENU

Step I: During the day, either with eyes open or closed, notice what is happening with your psycho-emotional processes.

Step II: Identifying: Pick from the menu of the aspects of consciousness one or more of the terms that fit your experience. For example, if you have a troublesome thought, call it a thought; or if you have a troublesome internal voice, call it an internal dialogue. In this way, you will be able to differentiate between the different aspects of consciousness.

Step III: Dialogue with the aspect. Ask the aspect, "What are you resisting knowing about yourself?" Write down your answers until nothing comes up.

Step IV: Notice what the aspect is resisting even as you continue to enquire.

Step V: Realizing what the aspect is ultimately resisting, allow the aspect to experience what it is resisting and then notice the **EMPTINESS** surrounding it and see and/or experience the **EMPTINESS** and the aspect as being the same substance.

Step VI: Stay in the nonverbal **I AM** level *prior* to the arising of thoughts and JUST BE (to be discussed later). This is the **I AM** which leads to the **NOT-I-I** beyond observation (i.e. beyond the observer-observed dyad.)

This exercise will hopefully open the doorway and help to stabilize you and to differentiate the thinking dimension from other dimensions.

10 ● ● ●

THE EMOTIONAL DIMENSION

THE THIRD DIMENSION
THE EMOTIONAL DIMENSION OF MANIFESTATION

The Emotional Dimension comprises our emotional states such as anger, sadness, fear, joy, etc. When a trauma occurs, if it is severe, it causes a painful experience, fixating our awareness and con-fusing the different dimensions of manifestation. The dimensions collapse, merge and become one rather than being differentiated. Let's say that somebody was molested by Uncle Bob. The intensity of the external experience creates a fusing together of all the dimensions—the External Dimension, the Thinking Dimension, the Emotional Dimension, the Biological Dimension and maybe even **ESSENCE**—all collapse and become fused, undifferentiated and solidified. When they collapse and become solidified, there is no longer any movement. The present time external world is seen as the past time external world through the lens of the past thinking, emotional and biological world.

WORKING WITH THE EMOTIONAL DIMENSION

THE TRANSMUTATION OF ENERGY

Transmutation can be defined as a change in condition or alteration, as in qualities or states of mind. In alchemy, transmutation (see Wolinsky (1992, 1984), *Quantum* Consciousness and *Hearts on Fire* respectivly).

QUANTUM PSYCHOLOGY PRINCIPLE:

If you are trying to get rid of feelings you are placing a judgment, evaluation and significance on them and are resisting them.

Most forms of psychotherapy do not focus on more than one dimension at a time. Problems arise because we confuse one dimension with another.

Quantum Psychology teaches us to differentiate between the dimensions and not try to solve one dimension's problems by using another dimension's answer. Simply put: *Meet the problem at the level of the problem.*

Furthermore, Quantum Psychology also shows us how to be aware of all of the dimensions. Below are some exercises which will enable us to free up and differentiate the emotional dimension from other dimensions, thus liberating our awareness.

QUANTUM EXERCISE

WORKING WITH YOUR FEAR

Step I: Recall a time about when you felt fear.
Step II: Allow yourself to re-experience the fear.
Step III: Notice where the fear is occurring in your body.
Step IV: Take your attention off the story or memory as to why you feel fear.
Step V: Put your attention and focus on the fear itself
Step VI: Now de-label it, experience it as energy, and allow the energy to do what it does, *without the intention of getting rid of it.*

When you feel afraid, your mind gives you many reasons why you're afraid. Normally people focus their attention on the story about why they are afraid. In this exercise you turn your attention from the story and put it on the fear itself. Where is the fear in your body? Begin to focus your attention on the fear itself as energy.

QUANTUM EXERCISE

WORKING WITH SADNESS

In this exercise, we will explore working with sadness. Begin by re-calling some past situation in which you experienced sadness. When you have got into it, then, move your attention from the story of why you're sad, or why you're feeling E-motional, to the energy of sadness itself. In other words, simply experience the sadness as a form of energy, without labeling it and without connecting it to the memory or story which produced it. See what this experience is like.

Step I: Recall a time when you felt sadness.

Step II: Allow the sadness to manifest.

Step III: Notice where the sadness is occurring in your body.

Step IV: Take your attention away from the story which explains why you feel sad.

Step V: Focus on the sadness itself, taking the label off, in other words, no longer calling it sadness, and, instead, see/experience it as energy. If any thoughts, impression, or the story comes up, take the label of of them and have them as energy.

QUANTUM EXERCISE

WORKING WITH ANGER

Step I: Recall a time when you felt angry.

Step II: Allow the energy to manifest.

Step III: Notice where the anger is occurring in your body.

Step IV: Notice the size and shape of the anger.

Step V: Take your attention away from the story as to why you are angry.

Step VI: De-label the anger, experience it as energy and merge with it. By merging, I mean to BE IT so that you feel part of it.

QUANTUM EXERCISE

PRACTICE FOR PEOPLE WITH SEXUAL FANTASIES
(FOR TWO PEOPLE OR FOR GROUPS)

Step I: Allow yourself to remember a past or present sexual experience, or create a sexual fantasy.

Step II: Take your attention off of the story as to why you feel sexual, and notice where in your body you are experiencing sexual sensations.

Step III: Experience the size and shape of the sexual feelings.

Step IV: De-label the sexual feeling and experience it as energy and merge with it.

Step V: Notice your skin boundaries.

Step VI: Take the label off of your skin boundaries and have it as slow moving or contracted energy.

Step VII: Take the label off the air, the room, the floor, your chair, the rest of the universe including your thoughts and have them as being made of the same energy.

QUANTUM EXERCISE

SEEING PHYSICAL DESIRE AS ENERGY
RATHER THAN FOCUSING ON THE OBJECT OF DESIRE
(VIJNANABHAIRAVA; SINGH)

Step I: Remember a time when you felt desire for something or someone, either in the past or in the present.

Step II: Take your attention off of them and notice where you experience this desire in your body.

Step III: Notice the size and shape of the desire and the feelings associated with it.

Step IV: De-label the desire and feelings, and experi-
            ence it as energy and merge with the energy.
Step V: Notice your skin boundaries.
Step VI: Feel your skin boundaries as made of the same
            energy as that of desire.
Step VII: Take the label off the air, the room, the floor,
            your chair, the rest of the universe including
            your thoughts and have them as being made
            of the same energy.

CONCLUSION

These exercises are a deliberate attempt to sort-out (differentiate) the levels of manifestation. In this way, we can liberate
awareness, which will hopefully enhance the subjective experience of freedom.

11

THE BIOLOGICAL OR ANIMAL DIMENSION

THE FOURTH DIMENSION
THE BIOLOGICAL OR ANIMAL DIMENSION

What is true at the biological dimension
may not be true at any other dimension

This dimension is your basic biological animal nature, whose most fundamental nature is survival. One teacher I worked with in India used to say that our whole lives were organized around four basic needs or drives—eating, sleeping, going to the bathroom and having sex. Or making enough money so that we could find a better place to do them in.

Quantum psychology adds two other pieces to the biological puzzle, a natural, biological merging response and a natural biological learning response.

QUANTUM PSYCHOLOGY PRINCIPLE:

A problem must be met at the level of the problem, and you must not substitute a biological need for another biological need (i.e., food for merger).

QUANTUM PSYCHOLOGY PRINCIPLE:

When a biological need is unmet and a psychological want is substituted for a biological need, it results in an obsessive-compulsive action, desire and reaction—*but no satisfaction.* For example, substituting approval (a psychological want) for merger (a biological need)

QUANTUM PSYCHOLOGY PRINCIPLE:

With the splitting-off and dissociation from any dimension, there is a corresponding loss of present time body awareness and the present-time external dimension along with the loss of the potential for stabilization in the underlying unity.

QUANTUM PSYCHOLOGY PRINCIPLE:

Psychology is caused by a dissociation from the biological core.

THE BIOLOGICAL CORE:
THE PHYSICAL MANIFESTATION
OF ESSENCE

The development of awareness of the Biological Core seems to be one of the slowest for two reasons: First, because it is part of physical matter it is denser, as compared to a thought or a feeling. Second, the present time demands of our industrial society force us to lose awareness of our biology and push us beyond what a body can do. In short, a combination of our psychology and the stresses of the external world force us to overcome bodily needs with psychological wants through the Thinking and Emotional dimensions. Overworking, toxic air and water, denatured food—not to mention the difficulties inherent in socialization—thwart our biology and cause greater dissociation. Modern day pressures put more of an emphasis on psychology and achievement, and forces a consequent loss of awareness of the body.

But if we focus our attention on our bodies they can yield a Biological Realization. What is Biological Realization? *It is the realization that your body is made of the same substance as everything else and that there is no separate individual body.* But in order for this explosion of awareness to be stabilized, and not just some kind of an experience which comes and goes, it will be helpful if the Biological Core itself were first stabilized.

But what is the Biological Core? According to Ida Rolf, the founder of Rolfing, it's the core of your physical being which extends from your cranium to your pelvic floor and which holds up your body. It is the awareness of the Biological Core, the felt sense of awareness of your biological being. The alignment between the gravitational pull of the sun and the earth meet through your Biological Core and combine to hold up both you and your body. For Quantum Psychology your Biological Core is the physical and biological manifestation of **ESSENCE**.

THE FALSE CORE AND THE BIOLOGICAL CORE

As previously stated, one of the tenets of Quantum Psychology is the concept of the False Core. Ideas, concepts, or fantasies which you have about yourself surround the Biological Core, and are known as your False Core. The False Core has underpinnings within the body which are mirrored in the collapse of your muscles. However, the False Core is an *image* you hold of yourself, which you try to overcome psychologically and biologically—*it is not you*. It is an "I" thought that the nervous system produces after the fact, that is, after an experience has already taken place. Why is it not you? The answer is simple: *Because "you" were "there" before the 'I' thought arose.*

Rolf used the metaphor of *sleeve* and *core*. She called the exterior muscles the *sleeve*, which could be compared to the compensating psychological identities which try to over-compensate for your False Core and which you *try* to hold yourself up with rather than allowing yourself to be held up by the gravitational pull between the sun and the earth through the Biological Core. Quantum Psychology calls this psychological compensating structure the *False Self Compensator*.

The Rolfian sleeve (compensating identities) is foreground, and can be physically and biologically experienced as sore muscles. But the actual Biological Core remains an unexperienced background. However, when aligned with gravity, the Biological Core becomes foreground and the sleeve background. What does this mean as far as our experience goes? It manifests as our living out of a true Biological Core and biological **ESSENCE**. It is experiencing, at a biological level, everyone's **ESSENCE** and our **ESSENCE** as the same. Life becomes an effortless process whereby you are *held up* by gravity. Like a fish who does not notice the water in which he swims, once you are aligned with gravity, the life process goes unnoticed and becomes effortless.

I met with Jack Donnelly, a Rolfer of some twenty-nine years, and asked him what Rolf meant when she talked about the Biological Core. According to Jack,

> You are dealing with gravity. When you are dealing with gravity, you are dealing with what Ida called, the primal core, which goes from the pelvic floor up to about the solar plexus, and the high core which goes from the cranium down to about the solar plexus. That is where they meet. . . .

> [According to Donnelly, Rolf felt that] psychology was formed by a breakage in the core, that the primal core and gravity are related to the earth, and that the high core is related to the gravitational pull of the sun, and that line between the sun and earth on a gravitational level is the Rolf line.

In Quantum Psychology, we suggest that it is the Biological Core (and it is a physical core not *only* energetic, as Yogis would say) that aligns our biology with the earth and the sun. This alignment is on a gravitational level through the vehicle of the body.

CHAPTER II

T he purpose of the Nervous System is to organize chaos.

Moshe Feldenkrais

The Biological Core is the physical manifestation of **ES-SENCE**. It is the bridge between the **SPACIOUSNESS** of **ES-SENCE** and the manifestation of biology held together by gravity.

The realization of the connection that goes up through the spine to the cerebral cortex and beyond ignites the realization of biological spirituality (i.e., the grounded experience that the body too is made of **THAT ONE SUBSTANCE**).

The more you are in touch with your Biological Core, the greater your experience of personal aliveness. Furthermore, the more you are aware of the Biological Core, the more making decisions becomes subjectively a non-issue, life, a non-issue and your psychology, a non-issue. You just are, things just occur. The Biological Core is the vehicle for the thinking and feeling dimensions. When they are aligned, there is pure being at a biological level, namely, **ESSENCE** and the **NON-VERBAL I AM**.

What holds back our awareness of our Biological core? In order to experience your present time body, past time body images must be dissolved. In this way, you can have your present time biology without being fixated on the past or your past time body image.

THE BODY AS AN ANIMAL

The following must be clear otherwise you will always have a problem. Basically, the body is an animal with animal tendencies. It is biological. The animal underlies biology and it is contains its basic survival instinct. Mom, dad, society (all of the externals) try to control and organize the behavior of this animal nature, whether by toilet training, getting you to eat at a certain time, or to go to bed when you aren't tired. Simply put, parents or society are trying to regulate the animal. But when our basic animal nature becomes socialized, the repression which results can be extremely unsettling. It is because of this dis-ease that many of our *psychological* problems develop. You can never overcome your animal nature. You have to unleash this energy. Acknowledge it, allow it to be there. It's very powerful, otherwise, the repression of it makes you crazy. The greater the repression of your animal nature, the greater the False Core and the False Self and its defensive substitutions.

CHAPTER 11

IT'S NOT HUMAN TO REPRESS:
BIOLOGICAL SPIRITUALITY

Through biological deprivation, trauma and the *splitting off* that occurs from the painful story of what is a narcissistic injury, you get psychology. When psychology is aberrated and dissociated, you get a high percentage of what people call *"spirituality,* which oftentimes is *spiritualization.* Biological spirituality is experiencing the body as grounded and being made of **THAT ONE SUBSTANCE.** Biological spirituality is getting that your body-mind spirit is one whole piece. There is no separate body, separate mind, and separate spirit. It is all a unity.

LIBIDO: THE BIOLOGICAL MERGER RESPONSE

Libido is the natural biological merging response, the drive to merge, either physically or at an external thinking, emotional or essential level. It has been greatly misunderstood. Libido does not mean sex. If someone says their libido is down, this is interpreted as meaning that their sex drive is low. But this is not what it really means. As the natural biological drive to merger response, the primal energy of the libido is actually a natural merging-separating energy. Like the tides, it is natural. When it is interrupted or stuck, we get psychology, and stories and explanations come out of the resistance to the natural merger-separation flow. Furthermore, because of socialization and the shock of the Realization of Separation, we resist having sensations within the body and accepting them as they are.

THE BIOLOGICAL FALSE CORES

The biological False Cores are different from—and yet similar to—those which are psycho-emotional. These latter False Cores are conclusions drawn from the realization of separation. They are processed by tracing back and, by staying in them, and dismantling the aberrated association which re-enforced them. Ultimately, you need to dismantle all of your False Core conclusions.

The biological False Cores are also part of the nervous system yet they somehow seem more basic. They are interpretations of the nervous system which have been passed down through evolution and hard-wired into it. This means they are earlier, biologically rooted, pre-verbal, and difficult to process. But you can:

1. Unfuse the *later* chains of associations which trigger the biology.
2. Acknowledge the difference in dimensions with awareness. For example, let's say I have a biological fear of the flu, for instance, as compared to a psychological fear that the world will destroy me. In the former, the biological fear is hard-wired into the nervous system. In the latter, the psychological fear is an abstraction and a distortion of a catastrophe that might happen in the future. Furthermore, it is a fusion of the thinking, emotional, and biological levels, and it is *NOT in present time.*

THE REMEDY

1. Acknowledge all of the dimensions.
2. Cut the chain of associations which are fused to the biological False Cores.
3. Go into the non-verbal **I AM** prior to the biological False Cores and their associational networks.
4. Breath into and *have* the experience.

WHO AM I?

The drive to know **WHO YOU ARE** is an inborn function, a biological drive, and learning response. **WHO AM I?** is a primary biological learning function.

QUANTUM PSYCHOLOGY PRINCIPLE:

Trances are the Nervous System's attempt to order the chaos caused by a shock. The Nervous System uses emotions, thoughts, and spiritual buffering trances to process and organize chaos.

BIOLOGICAL FALSE CORE #1

FALSE CORE CONCLUSION:

"I have no control." "There is no control in the world." "I am out of control."

FALSE SELF COMPENSATOR:

"I must control myself, control others and control the environment."

QUANTUM PSYCHOLOGY PRINCIPLE:

A False Conclusion about something can only result in an incorrect solution. And an incorrect solution cannot solve problems since it is based on a false conclusion.

CHAOS

Chaos occurs when we try to control our basic animal urges in order to follow what society and/or religion deem as inappropriate. By doing this, the external is fused with and internalized, and thus tries to control our biology. In this way, chaos and conflict arise, fusing with our animal nature.

BIOLOGICAL FALSE CORE #2

The next biological False Conclusion is formed by the newer brain:

FALSE CORE CONCLUSION #2:

"I am crazy."

FALSE SELF COMPENSATOR:

"I have to prove I am not crazy. I must be sane, clear, healthy, and virtuous," etc.

BIOLOGICAL FALSE CONCLUSION #3

FALSE CORE CONCLUSION:

"I am not safe, I feel no support."

FALSE SELF COMPENSATOR:

"I have to make myself safe or create safety and give support to others so others will give me support."

> QUANTUM PSYCHOLOGY PRINCIPLE:
> Personal psychology is formed to defend against Biological Deprivation, insure survival, deal with chaos, and restore biological equilibrium.

EXERCISE

STAYING IN TOUCH WITH THE DIMENSIONS

This is a practice that helps to develop the skill to stay simultaneously in touch with the outer world, your inner psycho-emotional world, and your animal nature.

Let your eyes close and divide your awareness in four directions:

1/4 to your animal dimension,
1/4 to the external dimension,
1/4 to your thinking dimension,
1/4 to your emotional dimension.

Note

As we go through the different dimensions it is important to keep in mind that we see our problems and solutions through our limited lens—or the limited lens of the person we go to for help. If I had a marriage problem and went to a priest, he might say the problem was spiritual. An accountant would say it was economic; a body worker, "It's in your structure"; a psychotherapist, "It has to do with Mom and Dad"; and a family therapist, "It's in your family context." No one system handles it all. Pracitioners—no matter what the discipline—need to perceive the client's level and what he needs to work on, and, when appropariate refer him to an appropriate person. This is a basic part of being a good therapist or spiritual teacher.

In the ancient Sufi tradition, a Sufi master would send individuals to different teachers so that they could get the help they needed. This demonstrates that not only does one system not work for everybody but that one master's teaching does not either. Sufi masters made the student's progress the center of their approach and work, not their own personal desire to teach.

This is client- or student-centered work. Unfortunately, nowadays when people go to a teacher or guru, *they all get the same techniques.* Furthermore, teachers, therapists and gurus oftentimes need (for psychological reasons) or want (for financial reasons) to *keep* clients and students coming. This "one size fits all" is a guru-teacher-therapist centered approach not client-student centered.

12 ●●●

ESSENCE

ESSENCE is what you were born with,
personality is what you acquire.
G. I. Gurdjieff

THE FIFTH DIMENSION

ESSENCE

In Quantum Psychology, the *internal* space that our physical bodies organize around, we call **ESSENCE**. **ESSENCE** is often referred to as an individual soul but this is a mistake. **ESSENCE** is actually a condensation of the **ONE GREAT SOUL**, the **VOID OF UNDIFFERENTIATED CONSCIOUSNESS**. In other words, there is no separate individual soul, rather just *one* soul. It should be noted that Gautma the Buddha's realization led him to go beyond the concept of transmigration, in which a separate, individual soul or atma, incarnates again and again. And in India, a person who is aware of **THAT ONE SOUL** or **THAT ONE SUBSTANCE** is called a **MAHATMA**: maha meaning *great* and atma meaning *soul*.

ESSENCE is a condensation of the **VOID OF UNDIFFERENTIATED CONSCIOUSNESS**, having the characteristics of that particular piece (of consciousness) with its memories, associations, and consciousnesses. For example, imagine an ice cube placed in a bathtub. It is the same as the water in the tub. In the same way, **ESSENCE** is like the ice cube and the **VOID OF UN-DIFFERENTIATED CONSCIOUSNESS** is like the water. The ice cube contains the particular characteristics which were a part of that area of the condensed water. And to an "I", the ice cube would appear to be a distinct entity, separate from the water. It doesn't look like water, it doesn't feel like water. But nevertheless it is made of the identical substance.

When we become aware of **ESSENCE**, we become aware of five different levels of manifestation: The external, the thinking, the emotional, the biological dimensions—and **ESSENCE**. Because of the False Core-False Self, **ESSENCE** initially appears and is (mis)perceived and (mis)labeled as emptiness, as in a lack. But once the labels are removed, once the False Core-False Self is dismantled, you can see that **ESSENCE** is actually **FULLNESS**, full of Essential qualities, such as love with no object, observation with no object, peace, compassion, unity, and **SPACIOUSNESS**, etc. However, *what is true at the level of* **ESSENCE** *is not necessarily true at any other level.*

ESSENCE is the **SPACIOUSNESS** that your physical body organizes around. When it is realized, this **SPACIOUSNESS** of **ESSENCE** is no longer empty (as in a lack), but becomes the **FULLNESS** of **ESSENCE.**

Essential confusion occurs because people confuse one level with another, especially **ESSENCE**. For example, you might have people in the New Age Community saying, "You must be unconditionally loving." The fact is that **ESSENCE** is always unconditionally loving but your thoughts and feelings are not, nor are they supposed to be. Problems arise when you try to make thoughts and emotions behave that way. It's not possible to be consistently unconditionally loving at a thinking or emotional level. Unconditional love and compassion are qualities of **ESSENCE** not of the thinking or emotional dimensions.

THE LOSS OF ESSENCE

The ultimate trauma occurs when the personality perceives itself as separate from its **ESSENCE**. This *splitting off* leads to a bifurcation point, where the personality splits and dissociates from **ESSENCE**, and repeatedly defends against the experience. This occurs because **ESSENCE** appears empty (as in a lack) to the personality who feels terrified of its own self and projects that terror onto others fearing they will annihilate it. Here we have the double bind. The personality is afraid to be in a relationship with others and **ESSENCE** and, at the same time, the personality *desires* the qualities of **ESSENCE**. This leads the personality to unsuccessfully look for these qualities in the external world where it is impossible to "get" them. It's like the old song, "Looking for love in all the wrong places." Furthermore, the personality is also terrified of the *quanta* which means energy packet stored up during this traumatic shock and fragmentation, seeing these energy packets as overwhelming and chaotic. When facing this energy, clients often feel it is so powerful, it could explode and destroy them and everyone around them.

The predicament of personality is illustrated in the fairy tale, *The Ugly Duckling*. The ugly duckling is treated as ugly by the outer world, thinks it's ugly, until it *realized*, when it looks at itself, it is a beautiful swan (**ESSENCE**).

ESSENCE acts as the touchstone or bridge between the ultimate and the physical universe, standing between what the noted physicist, David Bohm, called the implicate (BIG Emptiness) and explicate (condensed Emptiness) orders.

The paradox is that to the personality, the empty space of **ESSENCE** seems like chaos.

To help understand **ESSENCE**, it is necessary to realize that the personality consists of an accumulation of I-dentities created to ensure survival. I-dentities exist in a frozen pattern—they are frozen ordering outer chaos, and resisting the *mis-labeled* inner chaos of *emptiness*. In this way, the I-dentities of personality are in a double-bind, frozen between outward and what they misunderstand as inward chaos. In reality, **ESSENCE** contains all of the necessary qualities to organize chaos.

THE PROCESS

Before we continue let me define chaos: "The infinity of space or formless matter supposed to have preceded the existence of the ordered universe" (Webster's Dictionary, 1988, p. 79). I mentioned this because we must go into this infinity of space, which wrongly feels to an I-dentity like chaos, in order to enter into **ESSENCE**.

QUANTUM PSYCHOLOGY PRINCIPLE:

ESSENCE which is condensed VOID contains within it not only a piece of the COLLECTIVE, but it is also the VOID.

We might *imagine* that an individual soul exists at the level of ESSENCE, but it is important to see that there is no individual soul. There is only the one BIG EMPTINESS or the VOID OF UNDIFFERENTIATED CONSCIOUSNESS, which appears as condensed EMPTINESS to an "I" (also condensed EMPTINESS). In this regard, Quantum Psychology agrees with Buddhism which states that *"There is no individual soul transmigrating or incarnating from lifetime to lifetime."* There is only THAT ONE SUBSTANCE and when an individual dies, or when the ice cube melts, they return to the source.

Perhaps, ESSENCE is the last state that can somehow be termed *"personal"*—not in the sense of an individual soul but as a process which has certain specific qualities. Infants are fairly unconditioned and so they are very close to ESSENCE. If you look in their eyes they seem to have a sense of ESSENCE, which might explain why people *ooh* and *ahh* around babies—their ESSENCE evokes the open-heartedness of another's ESSENCE.

During the shock of the Realization of Separation, infants might have energetic-genetic proclivities toward one specific False Core or another. But at the same time, when the shock occurs, ESSENCE is blamed and a False Core label is placed on it. (Mis)labeled ESSENCE is then perceived as being the problem. It should be noted that the (mis)labeled SPACIOUSNESS of ESSENCE is seen as being empty, in the sense of lacking something, rather than as rich and full with Essential Qualities. Instead, it is seen as a lack and mistakenly blamed for an individual's *existential* pain.

Existential pain is described as a sense of internal emptiness and given the label of *meaninglessness, depression,* or *aloneness of life, etc.* The search for meaning is actually the False Self's attempt to overcome this False label. It can also be said that labels placed on ESSENCE subsequently become the alleged archetype known by Jungians as the *shadow.* For now, consider that all the things you don't want to know, namely, all the associations of the shock of the Realization of Separation, are blamed on ESSENCE or **I AM**, which gets confused with emptiness (as in a lack). The **BIG EMPTINESS** is part of **ESSENCE** though it is not perceived as such.

This mis-labeled **ESSENCE**, with the quality of **SPACIOUS- NESS**, is now emptiness (as in a lack), wrongly appears as the *repository* and the *cause* of all of our problems. In this way, the False Core Driver, which is the label, and our I-dentities are seen as "me" and **ESSENCE, I AM**, and the **VOID**, as "Not me". The *existential* crisis, in which life is seen as empty and meaningless, is really a misidentification. It only describes a label placed on **ES- SENCE**, which when it is de-labeled, brings into awareness the **SPACIOUSNESS** of **ESSENCE** with other Essential qualities. When **ESSENCE** is (mis)labeled, this creates a crisis which leads to organizing and giving a False reason, a False cause, a False con- clusion for the chaos caused by the shock of the Realization of Separation and the narcissistic wound. Thus, you are unable to experience your **ESSENCE** and your **SPACIOUSNESS** because they are fused with your False Core. And so your **ESSENCE** is now (mis)-labeled as your False Core and the reason and cause as to why there was a separation from your mother. This is eventu- ally trance-fered to everyone else, as well as the world and God.

ESSENTIAL QUALITIES

Quantum Psychology defines *Essential qualities* as *pure,* or as having no subject or object. *Pure* being, *pure* love, *pure* observa- tion or *pure* knowing—these are all Essential qualities.

WHAT ARE ESSENTIAL QUALITIES?

ESSENCE contains Essential qualities, such as love with no object, observation with no object, **SPACIOUSNESS**, compas- sion, peace, freedom, etc., beyond which is the No-state state or the Stateless state of **I AM**. Unfortunately, as identities are formed to aid in the our physical survival, the awareness of **ESSENCE** with its Essential qualities, as well as the **I AM,** begins to diminish greatly until it begins to go unnoticed. Observers are formed to enable the physical body to survive. With the loss of the Essential qualities of **ESSENCE**, we lose access to our deepest selves. The False Core-False Self and identities attempt to unsuccessfully cap- ture, externally (i.e., in the external dimension) what **ESSENCE** *is* and contains—and which we already are. It is as if the False Self identities faced outward looking for things such as love or _fill in the blank_ from the external dimension, which are doomed to failure since the False Self and its identities are collapsing the dimensions. These identities are trying to get from the external dimension that which is contained within the Essential dimension, searching for Essential qualities in the thinking or emotional dimension. But these other dimensions, such as external or biological, cannot experience **ESSENCE**. This is not their function. **ESSENCE** is outside of the awareness of the other dimensions. Only when we are in **ESSENCE** can we experience **ESSENCE** and Essential Qualities. But the False Self continues on a hopeless path to try to heal the False Core. It is only when the False Core-False Self is dismantled that **ESSENCE** can be revealed and stabilized.

To demonstrate the power of the False Core and its fusion with the **ESSENCE** an exercise is provided below.

BEYOND THE FALSE CORE INTO ESSENCE

This exercise will try to lead you through the False Core into **ESSENCE**.

YOUR ESSENTIAL CORE

What is your Essential Core? Your Essential Core is _you_ prior to the False Core. It contains Essential qualities of your core. Beyond this is the quality-less or _Stateless State of_ **I AM**.

ESSENTIAL DIMENSION EXERCISE #1

(GUIDED)

Group Exercise: Possible format for rotating group leader. Eyes closed.

Step 1:	Go into your False Core.
Step 2:	Notice the difference between you and your False Core.
Step 3:	Notice the size and shape of your False Core. (You can do this by stepping out of your False Core.)
Step 4:	Take a moment to notice the different chains of associations that are associated with the

False Core. (For example, if your False Core is "I am inadequate," then notice all of the different chains of associations that are associated with it.)

Step 5:   Notice how much energy and attention is tied up in the False Core-False Self.

Step 6:   Notice that it is this energy that pulls your attention into it, like a magnet.

Step 7:   Notice the **BIG EMPTINESS** that your False Core is floating in.

Step 8:   Ask your False Core (and allow it to answer), "What is it that you are seeking more than anything else in the world." (Now, you may not get a quick response but I want you to stay with it for a little while. Get a sense of what your False Core is really seeking.)

Step 9:   When you get a sense of what that False Core is seeking more than anything else in the world. Ask yourself, "And if I felt that *Essential qualities*, what would that feel like; experience that quality of **ESSENCE**. (For example, if your False Core is seeking peace, experience the peace.)

Step 10:   Notice what, if anything, happens to your False Core as you go into this **essential** experience.

Step 11:   From inside your **ESSENCE**, notice the size and shape of your False Core, as well as the **BIG EMPTINESS** the False Core is floating in. From inside your **ESSENCE**, notice the intensity of the False Core and the associational chains that it contains.

Step 12:   Have the False Core and its associations turn around so that they can "get" that what they were seeking is in **ESSENCE**.

Step 13:   Take the label off of the False Core and have it as energy, and from inside **ESSENCE**, notice that the False Core's energy and the **BIG EMPTINESS** that it is floating in are made of the same substance.

Step 14:   Feel that essential quality and your **ESSEN-TIAL CORE**.

Step 15:   Split your awareness in three ways: one-third in your **ESSENTIAL CORE**; one-third just noticing what, if anything, arises; and when you open your eyes in a moment, one-third in the room. (Whenever you are ready, open your eyes.)

ESSENTIAL DIMENSION EXERCISE #2

SEEING ESSENCE IN EVERYONE:

Step I: Experience the **SPACIOUSNESS** inside your physical body (your **ESSENTIAL CORE**)

Step II: Being "there." Experience another's **SPACIOUSNESS** within their body.

Step III: Experience the **SPACIOUSNESS** of your **ESSENTIAL CORE** and the **SPACIOUSNESS** of their **ESSENTIAL CORE** as being made of the same substance.

STABILIZING YOUR AWARENESS OF ESSENCE AND THE ESSENTIAL CORE

The awareness of **ESSENCE** cannot stabilize as long as there are lies, in the form of unacknowledged material within Identities. For example, if my father beat me up when I was a kid and I say to myself, "He was a wonderful dad," that's a lie I have to acknowledge and accept before the awareness of **ESSENCE** can become stabilized. Otherwise the resisted experience will pop up again and again, pulling awareness out of **ESSENCE-I AM**, etc., and putting it back into the False Core-False Self. Lies cover up things and that takes energy, the loss of which drains your awareness level and conceals the awareness of **ESSENCE**. The lies you tell yourself can pull your awareness away from **ESSENCE**, just as the external dimension pulls up your *uncooked seeds*. Things have to be acknowledged in order to have a stable, uninterrupted awareness.

QUANTUM PSYCHOLOGY PRINCIPLE:

In order to let go of something, you must first be willing to *have* it. Lies are the fertilizer (shit) that keeps the uncooked seeds sprouting.

QUANTUM PSYCHOLOGY PRINCIPLE:

Every time you believe a concept, the awareness of **ES-SENCE** is diminished.

To illustrate: At first your identities are foreground while **ES-SENCE-I AM** are in the background. As less and less attention is placed on the False Core-False Self, this shifts and the awareness of **ESSENCE-I AM** moves forward while the fixated awareness of the False Core loosens and recedes. When this happens, you lose interest in—and move beyond—your personal psychology which you realize is simply a lens through which the imagined self and world were viewed. At this point, the False Core Driver and False Core Compensator move into the background or just disappear. Finally, **THAT ONE SUBSTANCE** and the **NOT-I-I** move to the foreground and are clearly available.

TO EXPERIENCE ESSENCE AND YOUR ESSENTIAL CORE
EXERCISE

If you do not use your thoughts, memory, emotions, associations, perceptions, attention, or intentions, notice the Stateless state or No-state state of **I AM**. Now notice what emerges when I say, "And if you felt love, what would that feel like? And if you felt **SPACIOUSNESS**, what would that feel like? And if you felt compassion, what would that feel like?"

Notice what occurs when I say, and if you felt *peace*, what would that feel like?

In a moment I'll ask you to open your eyes and come back to the room. Notice the essential qualities of love, spaciousness and peace, etc.

THE ESSENCE OF ESSENCE

There is no self or imagined self which is separate from the lens it looks through.

The self is part of the lens, arises and subsides with the lens, and is contained within the lens itself.

The **I AM** is beyond this imagined self and its imagined separate lens. The **I AM** is even beyond the know*er* of the self-lens complex. In this way it could be said that the **I AM** is the **ESSENCE** of **ESSENCE**.

THE ESSENCE

To stabilize in **ESSENCE**, the False Core-False Self needs to be deconstructed and reabsorbed back into your essential nature. Why? If we were just to stay in **ESSENCE**, the False Core-False Self will still be functioning. This is what often happens to meditators. One minute they are in **ESSENCE**—the next minute, like a sling-shot they are in I-dentity. To a mediator leaving **ESSENCE** and entering the world is like a *smack* in the face. Therefore, we deconstruct the False Core-False Self and I-dentities so we can stabilize in the awareness of **ESSENCE**.

CONCLUSIONS

It is important to understand how basic pairs of I-dentities, which are formed to organize chaos and resist the trauma of loss of **ESSENCE,** resist and create unwanted states of chaos. What should be noted is that each attempt to organize the chaos is actually a resistance to an unwanted state. Therefore, it is the attempted organization of chaos which sends the I-dentity on an exhausting search to end this unpleasant state.

QUANTUM PSYCHOLOGY PRINCIPLE:

Each False Core is a strategy used to resist the trauma of the loss of being and the (mis)-labeled **SPACIOUSNESS**. A whole personality is formed around **ESSENCE**.

"To discover who you are, you must first discover who you are not." (Nisargadatta Maharaj).

THE PROCESS: MADE VERY SIMPLE

Step I: Write down those I-dentities which resist your **SPACIOUSNESS.**

Step II: Notice where in your body the **SPACIOUS-NESS** exists.

Step III: Enter into the **SPACIOUSNESS** and feel it.

Step IV: Notice how the **SPACIOUSNESS** seems like death to the I-dentity, but from the inside, the **SPACIOUSNESS** is calm, quiet, peaceful, and serene.

Step V: From inside the **SPACIOUSNESS** ask each I-dentity, "What is it you really want more that anything else in the world?"

Step VI: However the I-dentity responds, feel that quality of experience in the **SPACIOUSNESS** of **ESSENCE.**

Step VII: Next, have the I-dentities turn around and be reabsorbed within the **SPACIOUSNESS** which is **ESSENCE.**

VARIATION

Step VIII: Seeing the I-dentities in the foreground, stay in the background and notice the I-dentities floating in BIG EMPTINESS.

Step IX: Experience and feel the essential quality from the background.

Step X: See the I-dentities and the BIG EMPTINESS as being made of the same substance.

MULTI-DIMENSIONAL AWARENESS: DISMANTLING VS. TRANSCENDENCE

THE QUESTION

The most commonly asked questions are, "Why is Multi-Dimensional Awareness—and specifically, the awareness of **ES-SENCE, I AM**, etc.—unknown to us? Why aren't they available?" The answer seems to be that if all of your awareness is fixated on the thoughts and emotions that surround your False Core-False Self (for example, "I am inadequate," etc.), then there is no awareness left to be aware of **ESSENCE,** or **I AM,** etc. In other words our awareness is gobbled up by our fixation and cannot become stabilized in any of the other dimensions. And awareness that is fixated on a particular dimension cannot be liberated. But this tendency shifts, and awareness, which is chronically ensnared, becomes liberated. When your awareness is freed up, then **ESSENCE, I AM,** "**NOT-I-I,**" etc. merge naturally. You can't work on **ESSENCE.** **ESSENCE** is always there; the **VOID** is always there. But you can work on dismantling your fixated Awareness.

A REVIEW

As Nisargadatta Maharaj has said, "You cannot let go of something until you know what it is." Spiritual systems are often more into transcendence and going beyond than they are in dismantling things. In many *spiritual* traditions there is an idea that if I repeat my mantra enough and meditate enough, I will transcend the ego or mind, and I won't be identified with it any longer. This *spiritual* theory is that through mantra, yantra, or tantra, you can go beyond the mind or somehow change your *vibration* in order to stabilize awareness in **ESSENCE, I AM,** etc., without having to recognize how your awareness is chronically fixated. As we have discussed this rarely works, is confusing and, in addition, causes all of the dimensions to get fused and collapse.

Quantum Psychology knows that to go beyond your psychology and stabilize awareness in **ESSENCE, I AM,** etc., you might first have to own your psychology before you can un-own it. You first have to be willing to BE it ("your" psychology) before "you" can UN-BE it until naturally awareness itself disappears. The liberation of Awareness occurs naturally. Awareness can then be in any dimension, all dimensions, or no-dimensions. Eventually awareness goes beyond awareness itself as the **VOID OF UNDIF-FERENTIATED CONSCIOUSNESS** absorbs the "you" you call "yourself". Then the **VOID** ends, or **VOIDs** itself, and the **NAME-LESS ABSOLUTE** is revealed.

The question in psycho-spiritual circles is, Why is all of this good stuff, which I experience in meditation, experienced only for that moment? Why isn't it sustained and stabilized? "I" used to meditate for three-to-five hours a day for twelve–thirteen years. And what happened was, I'd sit down at about 6 AM—in India I did it at 3 AM—and after a period of time, everything got quiet, and all of a sudden this beautiful **EMPTINESS** would open up and I would experience **NOTHINGNESS**. Then, I would get up to go to work, and within a few minutes my life and all of its problems would come rushing back. It could be my girlfriend calling me, it could be the mortgage payment that was due. It was always something.

So all of a sudden, my stuff comes back. I may be a little more detached from it because of my meditating, but it definitely comes back. So I would go to see my clients. In New Mexico, I would work from 11 AM to 4:30 PM. At 5:30 I would sit again for meditation. Soon there would be a quiet **SPACIOUSNESS**. But the same thing would happen once I was out of meditation. My girlfriend would tell me about some problem and all my *stuff* would come back. Well, the reason it came back was because I had been given misinformation. Meditation is extremely good for giving you a taste of **ESSENCE, I AM, VOID**, etc. But it has nothing whatever to do with, and will not handle, your external, or your psycho-emotional stuff. This was not apparent to me because I had been told that meditation would do it all. I began to discover, that it wouldn't and couldn't do it all. No one thing can do it all. Formal psychology does not do it all. Spirituality does not do it all. Each has certain strong and weak suits but none is all-inclusive.

In Quantum Psychology "I" frequently refer people out to get what they need. For example, Quantum Psychology does not deal directly with the physical body, and so I refer clients to body workers. If you came to see me because you wanted to work on your life in the external world, I would say that you really had the wrong approach. Quantum Psychology has no interest in that.

A FINAL RE-CLARIFICATION ABOUT ESSENCE

ESSENCE is misunderstood as an individual soul, whereas it is part of the subtle body, and a piece of the **VOID**. To go beyond **ESSENCE**, you must realize that it is condensed **VOID**. The **I AM** is the **ESSENCE** of **ESSENCE**.

13 •••

THE I AM:
THE ESSENCE OF ESSENCE

NO FRAMES OF REFERENCE.
NO REFERENCES TO FRAME.

THE SIXTH DIMENSION
I AM

The **I AM** is *prior* to **ESSENCE.** There are two levels of **I AM**—the verbal and the non-verbal.

The verbal **I AM** precedes the False Core-False Self; it is prior to **I AM** *fill in the blank*, before any definition of the self. You could not say much about yourself without the verbal **I AM**. As Nisargadatta Maharaj says, "The only thing you can say about yourself is I am." The verbal **I AM** is part of the newer brain and since it exists *prior* to your False Core-False Self, it is the root of your psychology. Simply stated, no verbal **I AM**, no I am a False Core-False Self.

The non-verbal **I AM** is defined as pure being *prior* to **ESSENCE.** It is the Stateless state or No-State-state, the root, or as Nisargadatta Maharaj said, the *seed of consciousness*, without which there can be no individual psychology. It occurs when you do not use your thoughts, memories, emotions, perceptions, associations, attention or intentions. It is the ultimate uncooked seed. The **I AM** is the deepest of the Archetypes of the **COLLECTIVE UN-CONSCIOUS**. The difference between **I AM** and **ESSENCE** is that **ESSENCE** contains essential qualities whereas **I AM** consists of no thoughts, memories, emotions, associations, perceptions, attention, or intentions.

The non-verbal **I AM** could be called the **Essence** of **ES-SENCE**, since it is *prior* to any qualities and is a Stateless State or No-State-state. If you are not using your thoughts, memory, emotions, associations or perceptions, you are in pure being—or what Nisargadatta Maharaj would call the no-State, the Stateless state of the non-being being.

The non-verbal **I AM** uses no lenses or frames; hence, the non-verbal **I AM** has *no frames of reference, no references to frame*. But what does Quantum Psychology mean by this?

Most of the time, we examine our lives and our worlds through various lenses, frames of references, or maps. For example, discussing behavior using developmental psychology or Freudian psychoanalysis. Thinking about spiritual problems in terms of Judeo-Christian theology or Hindu reincarnation. Quantum Psychology sees these as maps which are not intrinsically true, but which might be able to point out where a person is psychologically stuck. However, they are still maps to be discarded, not believed. If you believe in the map, you take the map for the territory, and ultimately, you lose awareness of the **I AM**. Ultimately, all maps, frames and lenses should be discarded.

But in the case of the non-verbal **I AM**, there is no question of using maps or lenses. The **I AM** exists prior to any kind of definition of the self and there are no maps, frames, or lenses. No references to frame, no frames of reference.

One of Nisargadatta Maharaj's major tenets was that we should hold onto the **I AM** No-State-State and let go of everything else. This was his way of cutting through the False Core-False Self. When you were with him, the non-verbal **I AM** and **BEYOND** seemed to be palpably transmitted from "him" to "you".

The non-verbal **I AM** is the seed of the verbal **I AM**—Nisargadatta Maharaj called it the "Seed of Consciousness." Quantum Psychology would also call it the condensation or the by-product of the **VOID OF UNDIFFERENTIATED CONSCIOUS-NESS**. At this juncture, it can be said that the verbal **I AM** is prior to the False Core-False Self, and the non-verbal **I AM** is the seed from which the verbal **I AM** and False Core-False Self arise.

No I AM—No False Core

Without the verbal **I AM**, there is no False Core-False Self and no individual psychology.

Without the verbal **I AM,** the False Core Driver-False Self Compensator could not exist because whose would it be? The verbal **I AM** cannot exist without the non-verbal **I AM**. In many psycho-spiritual traditions one of the two **I AM**s is the end point. Nisargadatta Maharaj realized that when the non-verbal **I AM** became stabilized, it would act as a gateway or portal that would take you beyond consciousness itself.

QUANTUM PSYCHOLOGY PRINCIPLE:

The **I AM** is the seed of "your" consciousness. No **I AM**, no individual consciousness.

"GETTING" THE I AM, SOME GENERAL EXERCISES

One way to "get" the **I AM** is through "experiential" exercises designed to get you in touch with it. In the following sections, we will offer some exercises and it might be that one will be more helpful than another. Just remember that however you get in touch—even fleetingly—with the **I AM**, it is the experience that is important rather than the means of entry.

Also, to make some of the abstract principles understandable, we show them in the guise of a story or an image. But ultimately they are not images or stories. In fact, if you remember, our stories and images exist as a reason for our False Core. But just think of how a quantum physicist might describe something indescribable by saying things like, Imagine you're in a rocket ship traveling at the speed of light. Such a thing is impossible, but he uses the image or the story to illustrate his point and we will sometimes do the same thing.

I AM EXERCISE #1: PREPARATION

Notice that every experience has different phases. Ramana Maharishi used to say it was important to trace the source of the "I" thought. In Quantum Psychology there are four stages of the "I" thought: 1) arising; 2) maintaining; 3) ending; and 4) "Quantum-fying." Here's one way to "get" these four stages.

Step I: Notice an experience or something which is known by you.

Step II: Notice who experiences the experience, in other words, who is the experiencER or knowER.

Step III: Notice what stage it is in and name it (i.e., arising, maintaining, ending, quantumfying).

Step IV: Notice what occurs when you say to "yourself", "What knowER is knowing that?"

Step V: Notice that the knowER along with the known disappear into **NOTHING**. That is, you seem to go blank momentarily and disappear. This is Quantumfying.

The Bhagavad Gita says that it is important "to know the knowER of the field." When the knowER or observER is enquired into, the knowER or the observER and the knowN or observED disappears while the non-verbal **I AM** or **BEYOND** remains.

EXERCISE # 2: THE THINKER IS IN THE THOUGHT

Step I: Notice a thought passing.

Step II: Try to find the self that's thinking the thought and notice there is none.

Step III: Notice that there is no thinker or you thinking, that the *thinker is contained within the thought itself.* Realize there is just thinking, which does not belong to anyone.

THE OBSERVER IS PART OF THE PERSONALITY AND PART OF THE OBSERVED

A pivotal part of Werner Heisenberg's theory of quantum physics is the fact that an observer cannot be separated from what is being observed.

As you familiarize yourselves with Quantum Psychology, it is initially important to develop, observe, and to realize that you are the observer and not what you are observing since anything you can observe, you cannot be. But the next leap in the process is to "get" that the observer of the False Core Driver-False Self Compensator and what is observed are one solid unit. The observer is part of what it observes but Quantum Psychology doesn't stop with observation. Ultimately, you go beyond the observer-False Core-False Self complex and enter into **ESSENCE-I AM** and the **NOT-I-I**. The **NOT-I-I** is beyond the observer-observed dyad; it is Pure Awareness which a yogi would call WITNESSING.

Now, who is the observer? The observer is the ego observing itself. *The observer is actually a part of the structure it is observing and it too has to be gone beyond.* Observation, as it is presently being taught, by many psycho-spiritual systems inaccurately imagine that there is *one observER*, which observes and exists prior to the observED. They don't "get" that the observer is part of the observed and that *there are an infinite number of observers arising and subsiding with an infinite number of observEDS.* In other words, each observED experience has its own observer-observed. In other words, each experience contains within it its own observer which arises and subsides with each observed. In this way it often appears as though thoughts come up such as, "I love myself" or "I hate myself." But actually what happens—and this is the major difference in the Quantum work—is that both *the observer and the observed arise and subside together as one unit.* And then a new observer and thought or experience arises and subsides all as one unit. There are an infinite number of observers which arise and subside with each experience, and each observation or experience contains a different observer.

119

THE ILLUSIONS ABOUT THE OBSERVER

There are three belief structures or illusions about the observer, or that the observer has about itself: 1) that the observER is separate from what is being observed (not true); 2) the observER imagines that it creates what it is looking at (the observed) (which it does not); and 3) the observER imagines it came before or existed before that which is being observed (which it did not).

But as stated above, in Quantum Psychology this observer-observed dyad is only one step in a process of multi-dimensional awareness, a step which must be gone beyond for two reasons, 1) because in order to stabilize in **I AM**; and 2) because as long as the observer is there, the False Core-False Self will be there as well because the observer too is part of the False Core-False Self and part of the same holographic unit. This is why observer-False Core-False Self is written using hyphens as opposed to separate words; it is one unit. Trying to separate the observer from the False Core would be like trying to separate the smell of a rose from the rose.

To sum it all up, *one can never stabilize in I AM or go beyond False Core-False Self* as long as there is an observer observing it because *the observer is part of the system it observes.* Therefore the observer too must be dismantled.

MORE ILLUSIONS OF THE OBSERVER

You see and treat yourself the way Mom and Dad saw and treated you.

When the observer is fused with Mom or Dad, behavior and emotions are viewed as bad, as vices or sins. You think getting rid of the bad is *spiritual* when actually it is an internalized age-regressed re-enactment of Mom/Dad as an "outside" or "external" observer observing you as a child trying to get rid of what they label as unwanted behavior or sins. *Once Mom/Dad as "outer" observers are internalized, the now internalized mom and dad are mislabeled as the observer which tries to get rid of the "bad" and keep the "good".*

MORE ABOUT THE OBSERVER AND THE OBSERVED

The observer is still facing outward, toward thoughts, feelings, images, and people, the observer is part of the personality, though arguably, a higher part. This is a first step in the process to move beyond personality. The observer separates from **ESSENCE** and, in varying degrees, grows along with the development of the body and the personality. This fixated attention is a strategy to resist the trauma of the perceived loss of **ESSENCE**. The observer and the cluster of I-dentities called personality are a unit; they are not separate. *The illusion is that through observation the observer can be freed of personality.* The fact is that the observer is created as the physical body and personality develop. *The observer is actually part of the personality.*

This is a controversial concept, and we need to ask ourselves whether anyone has ever been able to let go of personality simply by self-observation. This means to enter into **ESSENCE** and **I AM**, the observer and the observed, which are made up of the I-dentities, called personality, must be dismantled to stabilize in **ESSENCE-I AM**. When this happens, the observer and the personality disappear, and the essential quality of observation with no object, or what Gurdjieff called *objective consciousness* or **I AM**, remains.

Stated another way, the observer and its object are reabsorbed back into **ESSENCE** so that the essential quality of observation with no object (*objective consciousness*) emerges. How can there be observation with no object? Because, at the level of **I AM**, the observer or the subject and his or her object merge and become one. Later, beyond this, the observer/observed dyad totally disappears, and only pure **EMPTINESS** and the WITNESS is left, in what Quantum Psychology calls the **NOT-I-I**.

To illustrate, picture a wheel. The hub of the wheel forms the center axis to the spokes. **ESSENCE-I AM** is just below this hub. The hub is the False Core-False Self and underlying experience of personality. I-dentities are the spokes of the wheel. Therefore, if you can discover the hub (False Core) of your wheel, which organized False Self and the I-dentities, dismantling of the wheel is easier. And **ESSENCE-I AM**, which is underneath the hub of the wheel, is revealed. This wheel metaphor, or getting off the wheel of the cycle of birth and death, or cutting the knot of the heart, is a pivotal for an understanding of Eastern tradition. For that reason, Quantum Psychology explores the major hubs (False Cores) of the personality, which prevent us from realizing **ESSENCE-I AM**.

In order to stabilize in **I AM**, the observer-observed dyad must be gone beyond. Below are experiential exercises designed for that purpose:

BEYOND THE OBSERVER-OBSERVED

The purpose of these exercises is to get "you" beyond the observer-observed dyad.

I AM EXERCISE #3

Step I: Notice a thought.

Step II: Is the observer giving attention to the thought, receiving attention from the thought, or exchanging attention with a thought?

I AM EXERCISE#4

Step I: Notice an emotion.

Step II: Is the observer giving attention to the emotion, receiving attention from the emotion, or exchanging attention with an emotion?

I AM EXERCISE#5

Step I: Notice an object.

Step II: Is the observer giving attention to the object, receiving attention from the object, or exchanging attention with an object?

I AM EXERCISE#6

Step I: Notice a person.

Step II: Is the observer giving attention to the person, receiving attention from the person, or exchanging attention with the person?

Notice with each circumstance if there is a giving, receiving or exchanging of attention.

This first step enables us to explore how the observer used attention in relationship to the observed, i.e., thought, feeling, event, or another person.

We can notice that not only do observers place attention on a thought, an object, or a person, but the thought or internal image demands attentions in the same way. The purpose of this exercise only is to go beyond the *observer-observed dyad*—let's continue.

I AM EXERCISE#7

Step I: Notice an image.

Step II: Is the image giving attention to the observer, receiving attention from the observer, or exchanging attention with the observer.

Step III: Notice with each circumstance if there is a giving, receiving or exchanging of attention. Notice that in order to "be aware" and WITNESS the nature of the energetic interaction between the observer-observed, one *can not be the observer or the observed.*

I AM EXERCISE#8

Step I: Notice a thought.

Step II: Is the thought giving attention to the observer, taking attention from the observer, or exchanging attention with the observer?

Step III: Notice with each circumstance if there is a giving, receiving or exchanging of attention. Notice that in order to "be aware" and WITNESS the nature of the energetic interaction between the observer-observed, one *can not be the observer or the observed.*

I AM EXERCISE#9

Step I: Notice an emotion you are having.

Step II: Is the object giving attention to the observer, taking attention from the observer, or exchanging attention with the observer?

Step III: Notice with each circumstance if there is a giving, receiving or exchanging of attention. Notice that in order to "be aware" and WITNESS the nature of the energetic interaction

between the observer-observed, one *can not
be the* observer or the observed.

I AM EXERCISE#10

Step I: Notice a person.
Step II: Is the person giving attention to the observer,
           taking attention from the observer, or exchang-
           ing attention with the observer?
Step III: Notice with each circumstance if there is a
           giving, receiving or exchanging of attention.
           Notice that in order to "be aware" and WIT-
           NESS the nature of the energetic interaction
           between the observer-observed, one *can not
           be the observer or the observed.*

THE KNOWER ASPECT OF THE OBSERVER

In *Quantum Consciousness* (Vol. I), it was emphasized that the observer also is the knower of the known (thought). In the same way as mentioned above, the observer or knower is part of the known. More simply put, the observer-observed or the knower-known are one unit, and are made of the same substance. This is a major quantum jump of understanding because experience can only occur if the observer or knower of the experience and the observed or known are "seen" or are "experienced" as different.

Normally we experience one observer watching the observables like, "I love myself" or "I hate myself" or images from the past coming and going., It appears as thought there is one observer or knower. However, with each observed known, i.e., "I love myself" or "I hate myself", there is a different and new observer or knower, which arises with each new observed-known.

THE KNOWER OR OBSERVER

To understand the knower or observer and its impact on attention and experiences, let us imagine a wall with 10 different portholes (like portholes of a ship). In each porthole there is a different knower or observer which sees a different version of reality. For example, let's imagine you are in a relationship and your partner shows up 10 minutes late for lunch. If you look through porthole

#1, the observer sees an inconsiderate person leaving you waiting. If you look through porthole #2, the observer sees a partner who is always late for appointments. The observer in porthole #3 experiences fear that possible there was some accident or mishap. If you look through a porthole #4, the observer sees a partner who is probably taking care of an errand that you didn't want to do so you feel relieved., In each porthole a different "view" and hence a different perception of reality.

What becomes obvious is that each porthole contains a different observer or knower which within contains a limited observed or knowledge of its reality. The appearance is that there is a single knower or observer that is looking through all these different portholes. The subtle fact is that each porthole has a different knower or observer. Simply stated, there appears to be one knower-observer you probably call "yourself" which knows all these different portholes. The fact is that there is a different knower-observer for each porthole. Each knower-observer can only observe and know its own particular limited knowledge. This means that the knower-observer of, "I like myself" only knows that knowledge called "I like myself." A different knower-observer knows and observes "I don't like myself." Within the confines of the knower which knows ("I like myself") there is no knowledge of "I don't like myself." Likewise the knower that has the knowledge of "I don't like myself" has only the "I don't like myself knowledge, not the "I like myself" knowledge.

Stated another way, each knower has specific and limited knowledge. To go further one must go beyond the observer-knower to stabilize in **I AM**.

Let's go back to our porthole metaphor. It appears as though there is one knower that opens each porthole, looks through the porthole, and sees and experiences a particular reality. Actually there are numerous knowers which appear and disappear each having different knowledge or knowing. *The observer and the observed, or the knower known, are one unit and arise and subside together.*

WHY CHAOS?

By imagining there is one organizing knower or observer which looks through portholes of reality resists the chaos of disappearance. Actually, numerous know*ers* with their knowledge appear and disappear, as a unit. These know*ers* with their knowledge appear and disappear just as what you call you, appears and disappears. *There is no-you separate from the experience of you!!*

CONSCIOUSNESS

What gives us this illusion of one permanent know*er*? Consciousness. Consciousness is that subtle substance that makes and tells us what reality is and isn't. This is not to be confused with **UNDIFFERENTIATED CONSCIOUSNESS** which is **EMPTINESS/FULLNESS**. This is differentiated consciousness. Years ago while in India, I worked with my teacher, Nisargadatta Maharaj. One day a psychiatrist and his wife came and asked him this very long question about good actions, bad actions, past lives, future lives, etc. He responded, "Who told you that you exist?" When no answer came from the two questioners he said, "Consciousness tells you that you exist and you believe it, if you understand just this, it is enough."

What he was saying was that each know*er* and the knowledge it has, is the same consciousness knowing itself. Consciousness tells you there is a subject called a know*er* and an object called a known **(I AM)** and that actually consciousness is both the know*er* and the knowledge and the **I AM**. Stated another way, if the know*er* understands that it and the knowledge are the same consciousness, then the know*er* and the known (I-dentity) disappear, because there can only be a know*er* and an I-dentity as long as there is a subject-object relationship or contrasts. Hence, the observ*er*-observed or know*er*-knowledge is gone beyond and what remains is **I AM**, beyond the observ*er*-observed dyad.

To experience this the following exercises are provided.

I AM EXERCISE#II

Inner World

Step I: Notice a thought.

Step II: Notice the observer of the thought.

Step III: Is the observer giving attention to the thought, receiving attention from the thought, or exchanging attention with a the thought?

Step IV: Experience the observer and the thought as being made of the same consciousness.

I AM EXERCISE#I2

Step I: Notice a memory.
Step II: Notice the observer of the memory.
Step III: Is the observer giving attention to the memory, receiving attention from the memory, or exchanging attention with the memory?
Step IV: Experience the observer and the memory as being made of the same consciousness.

I AM EXERCISE#I3

Step I: Notice an emotion.
Step II: Notice the observer of the emotion.
Step III: Is the observer giving attention to the emotion, receiving attention from the emotion, or exchanging attention with the emotion?
Step IV: Experience the observer and the emotion as being made of the same consciousness.

I AM EXERCISE#I4

Step I: Notice a person.
Step II: Notice the observer of the person.
Step III: Is the observer giving attention to the person, receiving attention from the person, or exchanging attention with the person?
Step IV: Experience the observer and the person as being made of the same consciousness.

THE STABILIZED I AM

THE I AM IS PURE ISNESS.

All states of consciousness emanate through the **I AM** and only exist because consciousness says they do. Actually, the state of consciousness and the knower of the state of consciousness are the same consciousness. **I AM** is a Stateless state, a No-state state and beyond the knower-known dyad.

No matter what experience you are having ask yourself, "What knower or observer is observing that?" Most people go blank and into the **I AM** for a moment because "they" go beyond the observer-observed or knower-known dyad

I AM EXERCISE#15

Step I: Notice a state of consciousness that you are in, i.e., confusion, anger, neutral, etc.

Step II: Ask yourself, "What knower knows this state?"

Step III: Notice what occurs when you look for and question "Who is the knower?"

I AM EXERCISE#16

Step I: Notice a perception of an object, i.e., a chair, a bed, a couch, etc.

Step II: Ask yourself, "What knower knows this object?

Step III: Notice what occurs when you look for the knower.

I AM EXERCISE#17

Step I: Notice a thought.

Step II: Ask yourself, "What knower is knowing this thought?"

Step III: Notice what occurs when you look for the knower.

REVIEW

1. The observer-I-dentity either gives, receives, or exchanges attention with thought, emotions, memories, objects, people, etc.

2. Each observer-I-dentity possess limited and different memories, associations, reactions, perceptions, in short knowledge.

3. There are an infinite number of knowERS or observERS.
4. Each knower has an I-dentity which is a unit of Knower-I-dentity.
5. Each KnowER-I-dentity unit arises and subsides together.
6. The KnowER and the I-dentity are made of the same substance, (**CONSCIOUSNESS**).

ATTENTION AND THE KNOWER-I-DENTITY UNIT

It is often difficult to let go of a tightly knit knower-I-dentity unit. Why? Because the knower gives, receives, or exchanges attention with the thought, emotion, memory, object or person. This attention exchange is the glue that holds them together and gives them the appearance they are made of different substances. Therefore to move beyond this the knowER-I-dentity unit is helpful to acknowledge the a-tension between them.

I AM EXERCISE#18

Inner World

Step I: Notice a thought.
Step II: Notice the observer observing the thought.
Step III: Ask the observer, "Are you (the observer) giving attention to the thought, receiving attention from the thought or exchanging attention with the thought?" *Wait for a response from the observer.*
Step IV: Now "get" ("experience") the observer and thought as the same substance.
Step V: Notice what happens.

I AM EXERCISE#19

Step I: Notice a person.
Step II: Notice the observer observing the person.

129

Step III: Ask the observer, "Are you (the observer) giv-
              ing attention to the person, receiving attention
              from the person, or exchanging attention with
              the person?" *Wait for a response from the ob-
              server.*
Step IV: Now "see" "get" ("experience") the observer
              and person as the same substance.
Step V: Notice what happens.

CONCLUSION

STABILIZING IN THE I AM

When this becomes clearer and you find yourself in any state
ask; *What observer is observing that?* This can move you beyond
the observer-observed dyad very rapidly and into **I AM**.

These exercises are designed to free you from the observer I-
dentity unit so that you can be in **I AM**.

In the final analysis, each know*er* has different knowledge.
There is not *one* stable know*er* but rather many know*ers* that have
motion; i.e., which appear and disappear. If we allow the appearance and disappearance to naturally occur without the assumption
that we have a definite location and have always been here (the
illusion of time), there is only **I AM**. If we resist and insist that we
are in a particular location and are this one stable organizing know*er*,
we will have pain. In the Stateless state or No state of **I AM**, the
issue of chaos and order never arises.

This understanding of the appearance and disappearance of
different know*ers* and knowledge as a unit which are both made of
CONSCIOUSNESS is something that may not occur overnight.
To give up the know*er*-knowledge, observ*er*-observed unit which
holds the knowledge of location, and to take apart the attention
between the observ*er*-observed dyad along with the know*er* that
knows the knowledge of duration (time), is to stabilize in **I AM**.

In January of 1979 I was visiting Nisargadatta Maharaj. He
was talking about birth and death, and I began seeing past images
of when I was a client in therapy, "experiencing" births and deaths.
He said to me, "Who is the know*er* of the knowledge of your birth?
I thought to myself, "Who is the know*er* of the knowledge of my
birth, scratching my head. Later that day, when I returned to see
him I said "I have a know*er* of the knowledge of my birth, so there

is a know*er* while I was born and a know*er* will be there when I die. There are many different know*ers*." He nodded and said, "Of course." It wasn't for many years until that realization was stabilized that each know*er* has different knowing; one which knows My birth, one which knows my death. Each know*er* appeared and will disappear and the **I AM** is beyond any know*er*-known or observer-observed dyad. It takes time to integrate the Stateless state or No-State-state of the non-Being Being which is prior to the **CONSCIOUSNESS** of differences and is the **I AM**.

REVIEW

THERE IS NOT ONE OBSERVER

In order to go beyond the observer and the observed, we must understand that each I-dentity has an observer. In other words the observer and observed is a unit. It appears as though each "I" arises independent of an observer and that the same observer observes all of these different "I's". Actually, each "I" has its own observer. What are we left with when the observer-observed are seen as one unit and made of the same substance? We are left with what the Indian sage, Ramana Maharishi, called the *"I-I"*. In the fourth way tradition of Gurdjieff it is called "the Real I." In Quantum Psychology we call it the Stateless state or No-State-State of **I AM.**

QUANTUM EXERCISE MADE SIMPLE

1. Notice an I-dentity, or experience that is occurring.
2. Notice an observer observing the I.
3. Ask yourself, "What observer is observing this I-dentity, or experience?"
4. Notice what happens.

EVERYTHING THAT IS FORM WILL EVENTUALLY
BECOME EMPTINESS AND DISAPPEAR.

I AM EXERCISE #20

Step I: Notice a thought or feeling you are having.
Step II: Notice the **EMPTINESS** which surrounds the thought or feeling.
Step III: See the thought or feeling as condensed **EMPTINESS**.

QUANTUM PSYCHOLOGY PRINCIPLE:

Everything that is **EMPTINESS** will eventually become a form and everything that is a form will eventually become **EMPTINESS**.

I AM EXERCISE #21

FROM THE FALSE CORE TO THE ESSENTIAL CORE TO THE I AM

Close your eyes. (With a guide.)

Step I: Go into your False Core.
Step II: Knowingly, consciously, intentionally, believe your False Core.
Step III: Intentionally choose for it to be there.
Step IV: Notice its size and shape and all the chains of associations.
Step V: Notice its energy.
Step VI: Ask your False Core, "What are you seeking more than anything else in the world?" Notice what emerges. Ask yourself, "If I felt that, what would that feel like?" Ask that until an essential experience emerges. When an essential experience arises, sit in it for a moment. Acknowledge this as your ESSENTIAL CORE. Just be in it.
Step VII: Notice the ESSENTIAL CORE experience that emerged. Now notice what occurs when you ask, "Without using my thoughts, memories, emotions, associations, perceptions, attention or intentions, what is this Essential Experience?" For example, if love emerged, without using your thoughts, memory, emotions, associations, perceptions, attention or in-

tentions, what is love? Notice the Stateless state or the No-State State which is the non-verbal **I AM**.

Whenever you are ready, you can open your eyes and practice being aware of five dimensions: the **I AM** and essential core, your body, and the thinking, feeling, and external dimensions. Eventually, you'll "get" that the **I AM** is also a concept, a universal Archetype, and when it disappears, there is only **VOID**.

I AM EXERCISE #22:

THE QUANTUM PSYCHOLOGY SHORTCUT

Step I: Notice an experience.
Step II: Observe the experience.
Step III: Notice what occurs when the question is asked, "What observer is observing that?" Notice you go blank because in that "moment" you go beyond the observER-observed, knowER-known, and experiencER-experience dyad, and into the **I AM**. This eventually might lead to the **NOT-I-I**.

I AM EXERCISE #23

THE I AM

(By yourself or with a guide)
Eyes Closed

1. Without using your thoughts, emotions, memory, associations, perceptions, attention, or intentions, are you a personality, does the personality appear within you, or neither?
2. Without using your thoughts, emotions, memory, associations, perceptions, attention, or intentions, does this personality that appears within you have form, is it formless, or neither?

3. Without using your thoughts, emotions, memory, associations, perceptions, attention, or intentions, is this personality always there, does it come and go or neither?

4. Without using your thoughts, emotions, memory, associations, perceptions, attention, or intentions, do thoughts, memory, emotions, associations or perceptions, appear from the **VOID**, disappear in the **VOID**, or neither?

5. Without using your thoughts, emotions, memory, associations, perceptions, attention, or intentions, what is a personality?

6. Without using your thoughts, emotions, memory, associations, perceptions, attention, or intentions, what is it that has a thousand eyes but cannot see?

7. Without using your thoughts, emotions, memory, associations, perceptions, attention, or intentions, what is it that has a thousands ears but cannot hear?

I AM EXERCISE #24

FROM I AM TO NOT-I-I

This exercise can be done individually or with a guide. Let your eyes close:

1. Without using your thoughts, memory, emotions, associations, perceptions, attention or intentions, is there something wrong with you, nothing wrong with you, or neither?

2. Without using your thoughts, memory, emotions, associations, perceptions, attention or intentions, are you worthy, unworthy or neither?

3. Without using your thoughts, memory, emotions, associations, perceptions, attention or intentions, do you have an ability to do, an inability to do or neither?

4. Without using your thoughts, memory, emotions, associations, perceptions, attention or intentions, are you inadequate, adequate or neither?

5. Without using your thoughts, memory, emotions, associations, perceptions, attention or intentions, do you exist, not exist or neither?

6. Without using your thoughts, memory, emotions, associations, perceptions, attention or intentions, are you alone, connected or neither?

7. Without using your thoughts, memory, emotions, associations, perceptions, attention or intentions, are you complete, incomplete or neither?

8. Without using your thoughts, memory, emotions, associations, perceptions, attention or intentions, are you powerless, powerful or neither?

9. Without using your thoughts, memory, emotions, associations, perceptions, attention or intentions, are you loveless, lovable or neither?

10. Without using your thoughts, memory, emotions, associations, perceptions, attention or intentions, is there no control, control or neither?

11. Without using your thoughts, memory, emotions, associations, perceptions, attention or intentions, what is control?

12. Without using your thoughts, memory, emotions, associations, perceptions, attention or intentions, is there safety, no safety or neither?

13. Without using your thoughts, memory, emotions, associations, perceptions, attention or intentions, are you crazy, sane or neither?

---

14. Notice the non-verbal **I AM**, the No-State-state. Now, being in that, allow your awareness to move further and further backward, expanding out. Notice the **BIG EMPTINESS** and how it appears to go on forever. Just keep allowing awareness to continue to go further and further backwards. Now, allow the awareness and the awar*er* which is moving further and further backward to be the same substance as the **BIG EMPTINESS**. When you are ready, you can let your eyes open.

135

CONCLUSION

From here we can appreciate that **NOTHING** exists except on a verbal or thinking level. The body and the nervous system produce "I" thoughts. The body is a condensation of the Quantum **EMPTINESS** and is, therefore, a Quantum event.

Without using your thoughts, memory, emotions, associations, perceptions, attention or intentions, what is love, peace, compassion, spaciousness. And without using your thoughts, memory, emotions, associations, perceptions, attention or intentions, what is **I AM**. Notice the Stateless state or No-State-state beyond **ES-SENCE** or the **I AM**.

14 ● ● ●

ARCHETYPES AND THE COLLECTIVE UNCONSCIOUS

QUANTUM PSYCHOLOGY AND THE COLLECTIVE

In Quantum Psychology, the Collective Unconscious and its Archetypes are seen as being formed by a condensation of the Quantum **EMPTINESS** or **VOID OF UNDIFFERENTIATED CONSCIOUSNESS**. From a Quantum Psychology perspective, "first," the **VOID OF UNDIFFERENTIATED CONSCIOUS-NESS** contracts to form the Physics Dimensions of energy, space, mass, time, gravity, electromagnetics, and strong and weak forces along with distance and location. This leads toward the collective experience of Archetypes such as gods, seekers after truth, personal growth, enlightenment, anima-animus, etc.

In this chapter, we will explore the **COLLECTIVE UNCON-SCIOUS** and its Archetypes, as seen from a Quantum Psychological perspective, and how they impact and are the "you" you call "you".

BELIEVING WITHOUT INQUIRING: THE RISE AND FALL OF CARL JUNG

JUNG'S ARCHETYPES

For Jung, an Archetype is made up of archaic remnants of the psychic history of the human species. These remnants of human experience form primordial images which are more than intellectual postulates. They are models from which all things of the same kind are made. In other words, an Archetype is a universal pattern or motif which comes from the collective unconscious and is the basic content of religions, mythologies, legends and fairytales. It emerges in individuals in the form of dreams, visions and fantasies. Each Archetype, according to Jung, has its own specific energy and is capable of acting upon the world.

According to Jung, Archetypes, which are a phenomena of God-like dimensions, are alive and functioning in the world. They are able to produce a meaningful interpretation or to interfere in a given situation.

ARCHETYPES IN QUANTUM PSYCHOLOGY

For Quantum Psychology, the Archetype naturally contains remnants of psychic history with primordial images. But Quantum Psychology *does not separate* the Archetype from the individual since both are created by the condensation of the **VOID OF UN-DIFFERENTIATED CONSCIOUSNESS,** which yields a creation of the Collective-Archetypical dimension. It is a universal description of an occurrence not separate from either the personal or the **VOID OF UNDIFFERENTIATED CONSCIOUSNESS.** In Quantum Psychology, Archetypes contain different densities of the **VOID OF UNDIFFERENTIATED CONSCIOUSNESS.** In Quantum Psychology, Archetypes do not rule the world or act on the world, as Jung suggests, but are *made of the same substance as the world.* Archetypes come from the same condensation of the **EMPTINESS** formed by the Physics Dimension which is still a condensation of **THAT ONE SUBSTANCE.**

In Quantum Psychology Archetypes are patterns which describe phenomena which seem to collectively occur within the human species. Archetypes are not mystical though they are viewed that way *from within the Archetypes themselves.* For example, all False Cores Drivers-False Self Compensators have their origins in Archetypical patterns which come from universal experiences within the Collective Unconscious which is a condensation of the **VOID OF UNDIFFERENTIATED CONSCIOUSNESS.**

SUPERSTRINGS

Quantum physicist, Michio Kaku writes about string theory:

According to string theory, if we could somehow magnify a point particle, we could actually see a small vibrating string. According to this theory, matter is nothing more than the harmonies created by vibrating strings. The universe itself, composed of countless vibrating strings, would then be comparable to a symphony. (pp. 153-154)

Superstrings can be seen as a metaphor and a theory because it unites, under one concept, a way to describe a unified field theory whose scope fulfills *Einstein's dream of a theory of everything.*

Quantum Psychology is not saying Superstring Theory is correct, since whether the concept is correct or not does not directly matter. But what does matter is that superstrings include all forces and Physics Dimensions. Thus, it includes all of the Archetypes as well as all you call "you". At the same time, it actually suggests how to "get" **WHAT YOU ARE MADE OF**. Also, regardless of whether Superstring theory is right or wrong, the forces of the Physics Dimensions of energy, space, mass, time, gravity, etc., are here to stay. And the Physics Dimensions and its forces are of major significance in *Quantum Psychology's theory of everything.*

In Quantum Psychology workshops much time is spent dismantling concepts, the most crucial being energy, space, mass and time. Why? Because according to noted physicist, Dr. David Bohm nothing could exist in the physical universe if it did not contain these four dimensions. Taking Bohm a bit further, we can see that there are other Physics Dimensions and forces. There is an electromagnetic dimension, a weak force radioactive (the earth), a strong force radioactive (the sun), gravity, sound, particle realities, waves, light and dark matter.

These Physics Dimension and forces exist, as do others, some known, some yet to be discovered. But given that Quantum Psychology has one foot in the world of physics, it is important to be able to; 1) identify the Physics Dimensions and forces which appear to be outside of ourselves (but are not) and are actually everything we imagine ourselves to be; 2) bring the concepts which are now called Archetypes, which reside outside of awareness into awareness; and 3) dismantle them. Why? Because they are outside of awareness and yet unknowingly affect and fixate awareness.

THE PHYSICS DIMENSIONS AND ARCHETYPES

The first question is, Why is this section in a chapter on Archetypes and the Collective Dimension; and second, why is this a part of Quantum Psychology? As Nisargadatta Maharaj said, "You cannot let go of something until you know what it is." The answer to the first question is that we need to dismantle our concepts about things which are not the things themselves so we can experience what is and go beyond. The second question focuses on the Collective Unconscious with its Archetypes, or better yet, the Physics Dimensions as the source of what we call Archetypes and what we call the personal "I". To illustrate, imagine taking a prism and shining a light through it. Depending on the kind of light and the angle of the prism, different colors are formed, creating a rainbow. However, it can be said, that the rainbow is still made of the same one light. In other words, the colors appear different, but this is an illusion—the light contained within the rainbow is what the rainbow is made of, and all the colors are made of **THAT ONE SUBSTANCE**, in this case light.

According to Quantum Psychology's understanding of physics, before the BIG BANG and the creation of the universe, everything was **NOTHING,** or **THAT ONE SUBSTANCE.** When the universe cooled the different Physics Dimensions were formed. Simply put, imagine energy, space, mass, time, gravity, electromagnetics, strong and weak forces as cooled parts of **THAT ONE SUBSTANCE**, all of them now differentiating and exerting a force upon each other, and interacting with each other.

Now, let us go back to our light-prism-rainbow metaphor and substitute the light with the **NOTHINGNESS**, and the prism with superstrings as the medium to form the Physics Dimensions. We could then say that the light was the **NOTHING**, the superstring was the prism, and the rainbow the Physics dimensions.

And so, it could be said that archetypes, as well as the personal "me" or "you", are actually made up of a different combination and interaction of the physics dimensions and forces which are really made of **THAT ONE SUBSTANCE or NOTHINGNESS**. In our metaphor of the prism (superstrings) and the physics dimensions (rainbow), we could say we are a rainbow made of **THAT ONE SUBSTANCE**, which imagines itself to be made of different substances.

THE PLAY OF THE PHYSICS DIMENSIONS

The idea of a play or interaction of the dimensions and forces is not new. In the Hindu Yoga tradition, they refer to the world as a play of the elements of air, earth, water, fire and ether. *Very simply put*, the forces, which they call *gunas*, contain *Tama Guna* (force) representing the inert force *Sattva Guna* (force) representing purity, and *Raja Guna*, (force) representing activity.

According to Hindu Yoga everything, including us, occurs through the play of the elements and of the gunas, to which, according to the Bhagavad Gita, we are all subject. Nisargadatta Maharaj once said to me, "Even the physical form of the Guru is subject to the play of the Gunas." In other words, we, our bodies and all we think we are, everything is subject to, part of, and made from, these interactions, but which ultimately are really made of **THAT ONE SUBSTANCE.**

Given their limited scientific understanding of the physical universe Hindus remarkably described these forces and elements in the best and possibly the only way they knew how thousands of years ago, through the use of poetry, metaphor, and myth. As we enter the 21st century, only our scientific understanding has increased and so we call them Physics Dimensions and Forces rather than elements and Gunas. But the understanding that it, the world, and all we call ourselves, are formed by forces and that the Physics Dimensions which are not outside of ourselves (but are what we are made of) are interacting, playing, and dancing, like a ballet or symphony has actually not changed that much. As Kaku (1993) explains:

Matter is nothing but the harmonies created by vibrating strings containing the Physics Dimensions of energy, space, mass, time, gravity, electromagnetics, strong and weak forces. Since there is an infinite number of harmonies, that can be composed for the violin, there is an infinite number of forms of matter that can be constructed out of the vibrating strings.... The universe itself, composed of countless vibrating strings, would then be compared to a symphony. (pp. 153-154)

THE I AM, THE ARCHETYPE
OF THE PHYSICS DIMENSION

Or as Nisargadatta Maharaj said, "In the beginning there was **NOTHING ABSOLUTELY,** and on that **NOTHING,** the **I AM** appeared (through condensation), and one day this **I AM** will disappear (thin-out) and there will be **NOTHING** again." This means that the basic **I AM** which is the seed of all we call ourselves, is an Archetype or a combination of the Physics Dimensions and forces manifesting through the Superstrings and which arise out of a condensation of the **NOTHINGNESS** or **VOID OF UNDIFFEREN- TIATED CONSCIOUSNESS.**

As mentioned earlier, whether string theory is right or wrong is inconsequential. What is important is that there is an intermediate something, *prior* to the Physics Dimensions and forces which forms what we call "us", and for now, we might as well, call it Superstrings.

THE INTERACTING PHYSICS
DIMENSIONS AND ARCHETYPES

The **NOTHING** contracts (cools) and forms the strings which act as a vehicle to form what is commonly called the Archetypes of the Collective Unconscious. *The ultimate Archetype being the I AM.* To illustrate, the levels could go something like this:

VOID OF UNDIFFERENTIATED CONSCIOUSNESS OR NOTHINGNESS

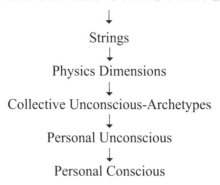

Strings
↓
Physics Dimensions
↓
Collective Unconscious-Archetypes
↓
Personal Unconscious
↓
Personal Conscious

The Physics Dimensions are *prior* to the Archetypes; and, hence, to dismantle Archetypes, we must dismantle our concepts of the Physics Dimensions.

This paradigm helps to clarifying the following points:

1. In most situations, with rare exceptions, the personal cannot be reached or stabilized in the **NOTHING** or the **VOID OF UNDIFFERENTIATED CONSCIOUSNESS** unless the *path* from personal to unconscious to Collective Archetypes to the Physics Dimensions and Strings through the **VOID OF UNDIFFERENTIATED CONSCIOUSNESS** is cleared (there is no path at this level, though for clarity we will use the concept. This concept too will disappear as well as everything, else in the **VOID**, the **NAMELESS ABSOLUTE** and **BEYOND**).

2. At our deepest level, the vehicle (psycho-spiritual system) we use to develop awareness is mirrored in the Archetypes which demonstrate stuck points in the Physics Dimensions as manifested in the personal (to be discussed below).

We are all made of varying amounts of the Physics Dimensions of energy, space, mass, time, gravity, electromagnetics, strong and weak forces. These Dimensions act as vehicles for the strings which, in turn, manifests the Physics Dimensions and its forces, and become all we think we are. Each psycho-spiritual path is fixated on particular Physics Dimensions. Each path is made of the

NOTHING or the **VOID OF UNDIFFERENTIATED CON-SCIOUSNESS**, and later become and unknowingly act-out varying degrees of the Physics Dimensions (Rainbow). And so even though we imagine we choose a path, the path might mirror and contain similar amounts of the Physics Dimensions of which we, the imagined chooser, are also made up of. The understanding then becomes clear that **SPIRITUAL PATHS ARE ARCHETYPAL.** Therein lies the problem.

QUANTUM PSYCHOLOGY PRINCIPLE:

You can never go beyond an Archetype by using, acting out, believing in an Archetype, i.e., you can never go beyond an Archetype **THROUGH THE ARCHETYPE ITSELF.**

QUANTUM PSYCHOLOGY PRINCIPLE:

If you are operating out of an Archetypical system based and organized by a Physics Dimension you can only act out the Archetype.

Do you know why you end up getting nowhere spiritually? You are acting out an Archetype, and an archetypical system can not go beyond itself. The Archetype condensed (Rainbow) can only choose, react, and re-enforce its own Archetypical patterns, beliefs and, in a word, itself. Below is a *very simplified* look at the dimensions and forces as they relate to spiritual Archetypes and paths:

AN ARCHETYPE CAN
ONLY RE-ENFORCE ITSELF

Very Very Simplified Examples:

DIMENSION & FORCES	SPIRITUAL SYSTEMS, etc.
Energy Systems	Kundalini, Yoga, Acupuncture, Taoism, Tantric Yoga, Tibetan fire yogas
Space	Buddhism
Mass	Sufi G.I. Gurdieff's (Fourth Way)
Time	Pagan Religions which worship seasons, Judaism, all religions which are organized around time.
The Strong Force (The sun)	1. The Sun as God 2. Sun Worship
Light Dimension	1. Rituals around light, waving lights, candles. 2. Light Beings 3. Yantras
Weak Force (the Earth, Volcanoes)	1. Earth Pagan Religions 2. Pagan 3. Earth as the Mother 4. Earth as a powerful volcanic Core 5. Earth as the Witness
Electro-magnetics	1. Seeing people as machines 2. Gurdijeff and his concept of Kundabufter
Sound	1. Mantras
Gravity	1. Rolfing, Feldenkrais

Psychology's greatest Archetype is the Archetype of personal growth. This Archetype is difficult to get out of since you cannot get out of an Archetype through the Archetype itself. These psychological Archetypes are seductive bottomless pits which act as traps. The Archetype of personal growth must be gone beyond to discover **WHO YOU ARE.**

Quantum Psychology contains two Archetypes that need to be gone beyond: 1)the eternal dismantler looking for something to dismantle; and 2)the concept that when all is dismantled the **VOID OF UNDIFFERENTIATED CONSCIOUSNESS**, or its Christian counterpart, the Kingdom of Heaven where pain ceases and we live in the **ULTIMATE FOREVER**—must also be gone beyond.

CONCLUSION

Why explore Archetypes as manifestations of the Physics Dimension? Because unquestioned Archetypes—be they spiritual or psychological are still condensations of **THAT ONE SUBSTANCE.**

In order to discover the primordial you, **THE SELF**, the archetypical representations, which we do not know are archetypical, must be gone beyond.

Why does acting-out of an Archetype get in the way of discovering **WHO YOU ARE**? Because the "I" which is doing and acting-out the Archetype is part of the Archetype itself and can only re-enforce its own survival. **YOU** are beyond all Archetypes or as Nisargadatta Maharaj said, "Anything you think you are you are not."

15 ●●●

THE NOT-I-I

THE END OF QUANTUM PSYCHOLOGY

What makes the **NOT-I-I** different from the **I AM**? In the **I AM**, there are no thoughts, memory, emotions, associations, perceptions, attention or intentions, however, there is no awareness of the **BIG EMPTINESS**. But when "you" stay with the **I AM**; it leads beyond the Stateless State or No-State state of the **I AM** which is the **NOT-I-I** where awareness of the **BIG EMPTINESS** is realized. Quantum Psychology calls it the **NOT-I-I** because anything that emerges is **NOT-I**, i.e., the observer-observed dyad is **NOT-I** and there is **PURE WITNESSING** beyond the observer-observed or knower-known dyad. Quantum Psychology calls it the **I** because there is still an awarER, which is an "I" or possibly what Ramana Maharishi meant when he called it the **I-I** who is **WITNESSING** and is aware. Therefore, Quantum Psychology calls it the **NOT-I-I**.

In the non-verbal **I AM**, there are no thoughts, memory, emotions, associations, perceptions, attention or intention. At the same time, there is no awareness of the **BIG EMPTINESS**. In the **NOT-I-I**, there is awareness of the **BIG EMPTINESS**, which is the unifier of all of the dimensions. Liberated awareness allows for all levels, while unliberated awareness collapses the levels and fixates awareness. The **VOID OF UNDIFFERENTIATED CONSCIOUSNESS**—which is not a dimension— is beyond the **NOT-**

I-I and it is where all the levels arise from and subside to. However there is NO AWARENESS or AwarER in the **VOID OF UN-DIFFERENTIATED CONSCIOUSNESS** (see Chapter XVI). For this reason, the **NOT-I-I** is the last touchstone before the **VOID OF UNDIFFERENTIATED CONSCIOUSNESS**. The **NOT-I-I** is where Quantum Psychology ends. (It should be noted there is neither a "where" nor a "location," but language is limiting in explaining what cannot be described.)

> QUANTUM PSYCHOLOGY PRINCIPLE:
>
> The observer and the observed are one and they arise and subside together as one piece, which can be **WITNESSED** in the **NOT-I-I**.

THE WITNESS

Going beyond the observer-observed dyad leads us to the **WITNESS**. The **WITNESS** is the one who is aware of the observer-observed dyad and is unaffected by it. It can be said that the **WITNESS** is the **NOT-I-I** since it does not have an identity but is *pure* awareness. In other words, it contains awareness of the observer-observed dyad yet remains unaffected by it. It is an **I** as pure awareness, being aware of the **BIG EMPTINESS** and yet remaining unaffected by the observer-observed. The **NOT-I-I** appears later, or is more solidified, than the **VOID OF UNDIFFERENTIATED CONSCIOUSNESS**, which contains the no-me of Samadhi, which is "where" awareness—as well as the **WITNESS** itself—dissolves.

THE WITNESS RESIDES IN THE SPACE
BETWEEN THE ARISING AND SUBSIDING
OF THE OBSERVER-OBSERVED DYAD.

The **NOT-I-I** is the last way-station for awareness. It is the destroyer of the imagined separation of the observer from the observed or the illusion that the observer is made of a different substance than the observed. It is also beyond where we imagine the observer came before the observed, which creates the illusion of time. The observer-observed arose and will subside together, and neither arose and subsided together. The idea of before is an idea of the observer only. In the **NOT-I-I** and the **VOID OF UNDIF-**

FERENTIATED CONSCIOUSNESS there is no before or prior, everything arises and will subside as one piece not in present time but in NO-TIME-TIME or NO-TIME-NOW.

NOT-I-I
EXERCISE #1:

TO BE DONE WITH A GUIDE OR BY ONESELF

Step 1: Notice what triggers your False Core. [In this Step we use the trigger as a vehicle or starting point to trace back.]

Step 2: Trace it back and sit in your False Core just for a moment. Do not believe the False Core but notice it, experience it and observe it simultaneously. (Here we begin to go just a little prior to it recognizing it is not true nor is it me.)

Step 3: Notice what triggered the False Core and trace it back. Go back and forth a few times. Observe this False Core which pulls your whole chain of associations. (Here we develop flexibility, the ability to BE and UNBE the False Core .)

Step 4: Now, notice the difference between you and it. (Here you get it is not you.)

Step 5: Next, go into **ESSENCE** *prior* to the False Core and feel its essential qualities.

Step 6: Notice the **BIG EMPTINESS** that this whole chain of False Core and its associations are floating in.

Step 7: Notice the energy that your False Core has. (Here we notice the **BIG EMPTINESS**—the **NOT-I-I**—that the False Core and its associations are floating in.]

Step 8: Take the label off the False Core and the entire chain while you notice the **BIG EMPTINESS** the chain is floating in.

Step 9: Have that as energy.

Step 10:   Appreciate that the False Core is just a condensation of the **BIG EMPTINESS** (or the **VOID OF UNDIFFERENTIATED CONSCIOUSNESS** condensing down).

Step 11:   See the energy now and the **BIG EMPTINESS** itself as being made of the same substance.

Step 12:   Notice what occurs.

Step 13:   Keeping that level of awareness, split your awareness so that part of your awareness is in the **BIG EMPTINESS** and another part can WITNESS whatever may or may not come up in the condensation of that **EMPTINESS**. In other words, should the **EMPTINESS** condense down and become a thought or feeling, simply notice what that is. Whenever you are ready, let your eyes open and have part of your awareness here in this room.

NOT-I-I
EXERCISE#2:

PART I

Step 1.   **WITNESS**, being aware of the **BIG EMPTINESS**

Step 2.   Notice the observer of any Identity and the Identity itself.

Step 3.   Being aware of the **BIG EMPTINESS**. Label the **BIG EMPTINESS** and the **WITNESS** as not I.

Step 4.   Label any Identity as I.

PART II

Step 1.   **WITNESS** being aware of the **BIG EMPTINESS**

Step 2.   Notice the observer of any Identity and the Identity itself.

Step 3.   Being aware of the **BIG EMPTINESS**. Label the **BIG EMPTINESS** and the **WITNESS** as not I.

Step 4.   Label any Identity as "I".

Step 5.   Change and have the **WITNESS** and the **BIG EMPTINESS** as **I** and the observer and the identities as not "I".

BEYOND KORZYBSKI

This exercise is called "Beyond Korzybski" (after Alfred Korzybski, the father of General Semantics), because he correctly saw that the nervous system organizes experience. Korzybski said that the event (quantum) level was not perceivable by the nervous system, which is also correct. What he did not understand, however, was that the nervous system is also condensed **EMPTINESS** and, hence, an abstraction of the Quantum world rather than the other way around. Metaphorically and anthropomorphically speaking, the Quantum world is an ocean and the nervous system a wave. The wave (nervous system) is only aware of the ocean from its own limited point of view.

But Korzybski did not appreciate that the nervous system was a by-product of the condensed quantum **EMPTINESS** or the **VOID OF UNDIFFERENTIATED CONSCIOUSNESS**. Because of this lack of understanding he could only claim in 1933 that **EMPTINESS** was incorrect and should be called Fullness or phelum. His misunderstanding was partly the result of the lack of scientific data at that time. Actually it is neither **EMPTINESS** or **FULLNESS**—because in order to call it that there would have to be an "I", which is a by-product of the nervous system to say it was so. Furthermore, he could not know, for example, what the eminent physicist Dr. Stephen Hawking would say in *A Brief History of Time* that in the beginning there was **NOTHINGNESS**.

NOT-I-I
EXERCISE #3:

Step I: Look at your experience. For example, if it is an experience of sadness, for example, take the label off of sadness and have it as energy.

Step II: Next, take off the label of energy, (since **EN-ERGY TOO IS A LABEL**). Then notice and dive into the vast **NOTHINGNESS** of the **NOT-I-I** and pure awareness.

THE NOTHINGNESS AS UNDIFFERENTIATED CONSCIOUSNESS

Another way of experientially understanding this is that the **NOTHINGNESS** is pure **UNDIFFERENTIATED CONSCIOUSNESS.**

NOT-I-I

EXERCISE 4

EXPERIENCING SEXUALITY AS CONSCIOUSNESS

Step 1:   Recall a time you felt sexual,.
Step 2:   Notice where in your body you feel the sexual energy.
Step 3:   Focus your attention on the sexuality itself as consciousness.
Step 4:   Notice you are the observer-knower of this consciousness.
Step 5:   Experience the observer-knower and the sexual energy as being made of the same consciousness.
Step 6:   Let your eyes open and experience objects in the room (i.e., tables, walls, chairs, etc.) as being made of the same consciousness as the observer-knower and the sexual feelings.

NOT-I-I

EXERCISE #5

ANGER AS CONSCIOUSNESS

Step 1:   Recall a time you felt angry.
Step 2:   Notice where in your body you feel the anger.
Step 3:   Focus your attention on the anger itself as consciousness.

Step 4:   Notice you are the observer-knower.
Step 5:   Experience the observer-knower and the sexual energy as being made of the same consciousness.
Step 6:   Let your eyes open and experience objects in the room (i.e., tables, walls, chairs, etc.) as being made of the same consciousness as the observer-knower and the sexual feelings.

QUANTUM PSYCHOLOGY PRINCIPLE:

To find out who you are, awareness itself must also dissolve. This puts you beyond the **WHO AM I** and even awareness itself.

EXERCISE #6:

AWARENESS OF EXPERIENCE

Step I: Acknowledge the experience you are having.
Step II: Notice that the Experienc*er* or the know*er* of the experience and the experience itself are made of the same substance.

Whenever a problem arises note that the experiencER of the problem and the actual problem have no separate individuality or self-nature. In other words, they are not separate from each other, they are made of the same consciousness.

CAUSE AND EFFECT

There are no separate individual causes yielding certain individual effects, rather the concept of a separate cause-effect causing a separate effect arise and subside together along with the "I" or experiencER which experiences them.

Stated another way, when you experience that the experiencER, the experience and the problem are one and the same and that everything is interconnected and made of **THAT ONE SUBSTANCE**, everything disappears or becomes quantumfied.

On the conventional level there appears to be causation. But because causation implies a separate individual cause yielding a separate effect, it implies two or more substances.

To illustrate this, exercises are provided below:

NOT-I-I
EXERCISE #7:
CAUSE AND EFFECT

Step I: Notice an imagined cause.
Step II: Notice its imagined effect.
Step III: See this Cause-effect as one unit.
Step IV: Merge all causes with their effects, or see cause and effect as a unity, which arises and subsides in the **BIG EMPTINESS**.

QUANTUM PSYCHOLOGY PRINCIPLE:

Since there is no separate self and no separate object, all there is, is the **VOID OF UNDIFFERENTIATED CONSCIOUSNESS**. By turning your attention around, the self disappears or is quantumfied. At that moment there is blank on the "screen."

NOT-I-I
EXERCISE #8:
NOTICING (WITH A GUIDE)

Step I: Look at an object. Pull your attention away from the object, past all concepts or knowledge of the object.
Step II: Notice the **VOID** behind you.
Step III: Notice that the perceiver is contained within the perception, and that there is no separate perceiver of the object, just perceiving.
Step IV: Without using your thoughts, memory, emotions, associations, perceptions, attention or intention, is the personality appearing within you (as **VOID**) form, formless or neither.
Step V: Without using your thoughts, memory, emotions, associations, perceptions, attention or intention, is there really a personality or just

these thoughts, memory, emotions, sensations, associations and perceptions floating in and out of you (the **VOID**)?

NOT-I-I
EXERCISE #9:

I AM

Step I: Be the **I AM**.

Step II: Turn your attention around and notice that there is no self which is having the experience of **I AM**.

Step III: Notice that the no-self and the **I AM** are made of **THAT ONE SUBSTANCE**.

Step IV: Maybe if you are lucky the **NOT-I-I** of pure awareness will disappear into the **VOID**.

NOT-I-I
EXERCISE #10:

EXPERIENCERS, RAMANA MAHARISHI REVISITED

All experiencERS and experiences have different stages. By noticing the stage, the experiencer-experience quantumfies. The four stages: 1) Arising, 2) Maintaining, 3) Ending, and 4) Quantumfying.

Step I: Notice an experience.

Step II: Notice an experiencer.

Step III: Notice its stage.

Step IV: Experience the experiencer and the experience are the same.

Step V: Notice they both disappear into and are **NOTHING**.

THE QUANTUM CONSCIOUSNESS PROCESS (WITH A GUIDE)

The Quantum Consciousness process is one of the highlights of this approach. These two processes, when understood and experienced, leave the practitioner in the Stateless State or No-state

state of the non-being being of **I AM→NOT-I-I**. Therefore, not only is nothing occurring; there is neither being nor non-being. Notice what occurs.

NOT-I-I
EXERCISE #11:

TO BE DONE WITH A FACILITATOR OR
GUIDE READING THE FOLLOWING:

Step I: Close your eyes and notice that you are the background of your experience.

Step II: Allow the **EMPTINESS** to condense into form and become an experience.

Step III: Pretend you don't know the form is condensed **EMPTINESS**.

Step IV: Be aware that the form is condensed background or **EMPTINESS**.

Step V: Turn your attention around and notice what, <u>if anything</u>, is doing this.

NOT-I-I
EXERCISE #12:

THIS FORMAT IS SUGGESTED FOR USE BY A
GROUP FACILITATOR. WITH EYES CLOSED:

Step I: Be the background of your experience.

Step II: Notice that the background is **EMPTINESS** and the foreground, you're looking into, to be thinned-out **EMPTINESS**.

Step III: Pretend you don't know the background is **EMPTINESS**, and the **EMPTINESS** in the foreground is thinned-out form.

Step IV: Allow the **EMPTINESS** of the background and the **EMPTINESS** of the foreground and the "you" which is noticing this to be experienced as the same **EMPTINESS**.

NOT-I-I
EXERCISE #13:

TO BE READ OUT LOUD BY GROUP FACILITATOR.

Step I: Experience "yourself" as the background of an experience and the experience as foreground.

Step II: Notice the observer of the experience.

Step III: Notice that you are the background of the observer.

Step IV: Notice that the observer and the experience it observes is foreground.

Step V: Condense the background making it into the experience in the foreground.

Step VI: Thin-out the observer making it background.

Step VII: Make any "you" that is being experienced in the foreground into the background by thinning it out.

Step IX: Turn your attention around and notice there is *no you* doing this exercise just **EMPTINESS**.

QUANTUM CONTEMPLATIONS

I. Could there be an experience if there were no consciousness which knows it is an experience?

II. Contemplate that **EMPTINESS** is thinned-out something, and the something is condensed **EMPTINESS**.

III. Contemplate the **NOTHING** becomes thoughts, feelings, images, chairs, etc.

IV. Contemplate the **NOTHING** becomes this "YOU", and the **NOTHING** becomes this not **YOU.**

V. Contemplate everything (experiences, actions, the movement of the eyes, smells, understanding) is made of and by that **EMPTINESS** and occurs or doesn't occur through or by **EMPTINESS**.

NOT-I-I
THE CONCLUDING EXERCISE #14
(WITH A GUIDE)

Step I: Without using your thoughts, memory, emotions, associations, perceptions, attention or intentions, are you a man, woman or neither?

Step II: Without using your thoughts, memory, emotions, associations, perceptions, attention or intentions, are you a personality, not a personality or neither?

Step III: Without using your thoughts, memory, emotions, associations, perceptions, attention or intentions, do you exist, not exist or neither?

Step IV: Notice the Stateless State or No-State state of **I AM**.

Step V: Allow "your" awareness to move or fall or expand outward and/or backward noticing the **BIG EMPTINESS**.

Step VI: Notice how the **EMPTINESS** appears to go on forever.

WELCOME TO THE **NOT-I-I**

16 •••

THE VOID OF UNDIFFERENTIATED CONSCIOUSNESS

*Non-locality is the
cornerstone of quantum physics.*
Niels Bohr

QUANTUM PSYCHOLOGY PRINCIPLE:

Awareness is a condensation of the **VOID OF UNDIF-FERENTIATED CONSCIOUSNESS**. It is the condensed **VOID** being aware of itself. When awareness thins-out and disappears into the **VOID OF UNDIFFERENTIATED CONSCIOUSNESS**, all ideas or experiences and experiencERs of the **VOID OF UNDIFFERENTIATED CONSCIOUSNESS** disappear, including awareness itself, then there is no-me referred to in Sanskrit **SAMADHI**.

THE VOID

The **EMPTINESS** of the **VOID** is a hallmark of most forms of Buddhism. The **VOID OF UNDIFFERENTIATED CON-SCIOUSNESS** as **THAT** or **EMPTINESS**, or **THAT "EVERY-**

THING" of which everything is made of, is the **VOID OF UN-DIFFERENTIATED CONSCIOUSNESS,** i.e., not only thoughts, memory, emotions associations, perceptions, attention or intensions, but also chairs, people and bodies, etc., and represents the foundation of the "realization" in all yoga, The Buddhist Heart Sutra says, **EMPTINESS** is none other than form, form is none other than **EMPTINESS.** It could be said in Tantric Yoga that everything is made of **(UNDIFFERENTIATED) CONSCIOUSNESS** and form is condensed **(UNDIFFERENTIATED) CONSCIOUSNESS.** Einstein said Everything is made of **EMPTINESS**, and form is condensed **EMPTINESS.** From the dimension of pure awareness of the **NOT-I-I**, it can be said that the **EMPTINESS** or **UNDIFFERENTIATED CONSCIOUSNESS** condenses down and becomes form and the form thins-out and becomes **EMPTINESS.** This is the movement or pulsation which in Sanskrit and in pure Tantric Yoga is called *Spanda* which translates as the divine pulsation or the divine throb.

The **VOID OF UNDIFFERENTIATED CONSCIOUSNESS** is the ground of being, it is prior to the Archetypes of the **COLLECTIVE UNCONSCIOUSNESS** prior to energy, space, mass, time, light, gravity, strong and weak forces and all physics dimensions and forces, both physical and non-physical. The **VOID OF UNDIFFERENTIATED CONSCIOUSNESS** is prior to superstrings, and it is the **VOID** OF **UNDIFFERENTIATED CONSCIOUSNESS** which appears as concepts and forms, and what we call our physical universe.

In order to clarify, differentiated consciousness knows itself and "I" and "thou", or subject and object. The **VOID** is **UNDIFFERENTIATED CONSCIOUSNESS** does not know itself. The **VOID** is not a dimension.

The **VOID OF UNDIFFERENTIATED CONSCIOUSNESS** is pure **NOTHINGNESS** or better said no-thing-ness (although it is not empty as we might "think" of it), and "here" even awareness itself disappears within it. In this way there is no separate "I", "me", "mine" "self", or even awareness itself. There is not even **CONSCIOUSNESS** in the **VOID OF UNDIFFERENTIATED CONSCIOUSNESS** because there would have to be a separate "I" to say it was so.

QUANTUM PSYCHOLOGY PRINCIPLE:

You can never say what the **VOID** is, you can only say what it isn't. When asked, Who are you? Nisargadatta Maharaj used to reply, "Nothing perceivable or conceivable."

The **VOID** in Buddhism is the same as the **SELF** in Hindu Yoga, **UNDIFFERENTIATED CONSCIOUSNESS** in Kashmier Shavism, **GOD** in the Judaic-Christian world, and **ALLAH** in the Moslem world. The **THAT** (**VOID, SELF, CONSCIOUSNESS, GOD, ALLAH**, etc.) has no will, volition, preferences, plan, lessons, etc.

This understanding of will, preferences, plans, wants, etc., is anthropomorphic. These are ideas of a nervous system projected onto **THAT ONE SUBSTANCE**, which has no nervous system.

QUANTUM PSYCHOLOGY PRINCIPLE:

The **NOT-I-I** can be aware of the **VOID OF UNDIFFER- ENTIATED CONSCIOUSNESS**, but the **VOID OF UNDIFFERENTIATED CONSCIOUSNESS** cannot know itself or be aware of itself because there is no "I" or awareness with which to know it. This is why awareness itself disappears when touching the **VOID**.

QUANTUM PSYCHOLOGY PRINCIPLE:

The mind's entire reality and alleged existence are based on an illusory or nonexistent split between the primordial **VOID OF UNDIFFERENTIATED CONSCIOUSNESS** (the ocean) and the "I" thought (wave)

It should be noted that this "view" of a contraction and expansion of the **VOID OF UNDIFFERENTIATED CONSCIOUS- NESS** are merely an inference, or after the fact description arising within awareness or an "I". Actually from the **VOID OF UNDIF- FERENTIATED CONSCIOUSNESS**, there is neither expansion or contraction, neither form nor emptiness:.

161

*In actuality, **NOTHING IS.***
Nisargadatta Maharaj

The Mind is de-void of Mind.
H. H. Dalai Lama

QUANTUM PSYCHOLOGY PRINCIPLE:

The **VOID OF UNDIFFERENTIATED CONSCIOUS-NESS** is the mind, the mind is the **VOID OF UNDIFFERENTIATED CONSCIOUSNESS.**

THE VOID

GUIDED EXERCISE:

THE VOID OF UNDIFFERENTIATED CONSCIOUSNESS

(With a Guide)

Let your eyes close.

Step 1:   Go into your False Core.

Step 2:   Knowingly, consciously and intentionally believe your False Core.

Step 3:   Intentionally choose for it to be there.

Step 4:   Notice the size and shape of your False Core and all the chains of associations.

Step 5:   Notice how much energy is in that False Core.

Step 6:   Ask the False Core, What are you seeking more than anything else in the world? As you get an answer to that, notice what experience emerges as you continue to ask and if I felt that, what would that feel like? Continue to ask that until you get a sense of something emerging that is **ESSENTIAL**, and sit in it for a moment. Acknowledge this as your **ESSENTIAL CORE.** Just be in that.

Step 7:   Notice the sense of **I AM**, without using thoughts, memory, emotions, associations, perceptions, attention or intentions.

Step 8:   Allow your awareness to move, fall, or expand further and further "backward," and

162

notice the **BIG EMPTINESS**, which appears to go on forever.

Step 9: Being the awar<u>ER</u> of the BIG EMPTINESS. Allow your awareness and the BIG EMPTINESS to be as made of the **SAME SUBSTANCE**.

OR

Step 9A: <u>Variation</u>: Notice what occurs when "I" (the guide) says, "What awar<u>ER</u> is awaring this."

CONCLUSION

THE END OF QUANTUM PSYCHOLOGY

Quantum Psychology ends in the **NOT-I-I**, in the **VOID OF UNDIFFERENTIATED CONSCIOUSNESS** there is no awarER or awareness and hence there is no Quantum Psychology.

As "you" go into the deepest levels of the **VOID**, there is no "I" to have a psychology, and no energy, space, mass, time, distance, location, etc. In short, no Physics Dimension. There is no Quantum Psychology either because everything disappears.

With the disappearance of the awar<u>ER</u> and awareness, there is only **THAT ONE SUBSTANCE**.

The thing to re-member is that it really isn't up to a "you", that it is not personal, there is no separate individual doer. There is only **THAT ONE SUBSTANCE** and **YOU ARE THAT**.

17 ●●●

THE NAMELESS ABSOLUTE

There is no birth—
There is no death—
There is no person—
It is all a concept—
*It is all an **illusion.***

Nisargadatta Maharaj
to Stephen Wolinsky, June 1980

The above was the most important statement Nisargadatta Maharaj ever made to "me". To appreciate its depth we will first explore the **NAMELESS ABSOLUTE** , **"BEYOND"** the **VOID**. (Please note that this discussion requires the use of frequent quotation marks because language does not permit explanation without using "I", "you", "we" or "self" and "other".)

First, "I" would like to discuss how the **NAMELESS ABSOLUTE** began to appear to "me". In 1977 1 had the opportunity to go with Swami Muktananda to Shirdi, the site of the Samadhi shrine of Shirdi Sai Baba who died in 1918. Shirdi Sai Baba is regarded in India as one of its greatest Saints. While I was there, I bought a ring, which I had blessed at his shrine. I wore the ring only for my usual routine of meditation.

While "I" meditated each day. Quite unexpectedly, I began to feel as though I were being sucked into a spiraling vortex. I was left both breathless and beyond. I neither knew what it was nor was there anyone to guide me since at this time in history Gurus did not offer such individualized guidance. It freaked me out and I gave the ring as a gift to Swami Muktanada. But the memory of those experiences haunted me for twelve years and I regretted my decision to give the ring away. Then, in 1990, this experience began to be repeated. It would suddenly re-appear for hours at a time and then disappear. No words can even begin to describe what happened because in this "state," even the **VOID** itself seemed inconsequential.

What "I" realized was that there is not one **VOID** but an infinite number of **VOID** universes. Buddhism states that **EMPTINESS** is form and form is **EMPTINESS**, which is true within one **VOID** universe. To go beyond that, you have to go beyond the infinite number of **VOID** universes. In Buddhism the **VOID** universes are the Buddha fields, or you can say each **VOID** universe is a Buddha. Each identity has its own **VOID** universe. Every experience has a **VOID** that it is floating in. In Quantum Physics, the **VOID** universes can be likened to Parallel Universes.

You could call the **NAMELESS ABSOLUTE** the **SUPREME WITNESS** (if you are into Hindu yoga), or the Buddha fields (If you are into Buddhism) because the **VOID**s reside within the **NAMELESS ABSOLUTE**. Soon the **VOID**s disappear like burning oil wells that are contained within the desert, **(NAMELESS ABSOLUTE)** and only the **NAMELESS ABSOLUTE** remained.

The space between the **VOID** universes (**VOID**s) is the **NAMELESS ABSOLUTE**.

The **NAMELESS ABSOLUTE**, being beyond awareness or the **VOID**, is indescribable. But within the **NAMELESS ABSOLUTE** appears an infinite number of **VOID** universes. Some **VOID** universes contain the Physics Dimensions of energy, space, mass, time, distance and location as well as expansions and contractions which create the **I AM**, some do not. The **NAMELESS ABSOLUTE** is beyond the **VOID**. It is indestructible. "I" am only able to talk about it as a *luck out*, which is maybe what **GRACE** is—the **NAMELESS ABSOLUTE** revealing itself.

QUANTUM PSYCHOLOGY PRINCIPLE:

The most powerful Archetypes in "our" **VOID** universe, is the collective concept of **I AM** and of **GOD**.

The concept of God and a seeker after God or truth are Archetypes of such magnitude that it impacts practically everyone in the world. Most religions are based on an omnipresent God who somehow rules the universe.

QUANTUM PSYCHOLOGY PRINCIPLE:

The near impossibility of finding out **WHO YOU ARE** is because Guru-disciple and religions are models of realization. These models are Archetypes contained within and exist within one **VOID** universe only. To seek God is to act out an archetype within a **VOID** universe.

EXERCISE

THE NAMELESS ABSOLUTE (TO BE GUIDED)

Eyes closed.

Notice a concept you have about the **VOID**. Notice the size and shape of the concept. Let your awareness expand until the **VOID** ends and notice the **VOID** that that concept is floating in. Allow the label called **VOID** as **VOID** to dissolve and notice what happens. Notice a concept that you have about yourself. Notice the size and shape of the concept you have about this "you" as a "self." Notice the **EMPTINESS** in which that concept of you as a self is floating. Extend out, noticing the size and shape, of the **VOID** that it is floating in until the **VOID** reaches an end. Allow the label called the **VOID** to dissolve and notice what, if anything, is underneath there. Notice the experience called "I am doing something" or "I am not doing something," and notice the size and shape of that concept.

Notice the size of the **EMPTINESS** in which that **VOID** or concept of doing or not doing is floating. Allow the label called the **VOID** to dissolve and notice what, if anything, is underneath that. Notice the concept you have about perfection or imperfection. Notice the **VOID** universe that that concept is floating in or appears to be floating in. Allow the label called **VOID** universe in which a concept of perfection or imperfection is floating to dissolve and notice the **NAMELESS ABSOLUTE** underneath it. Notice the concept called worthless or worthy or not important or not valuable or very valuable and notice that concept. Notice the **VOID** universe that that is floating in. Allow the label called **VOID** universe to dissolve and notice the **NAMELESS ABSOLUTE** underneath it. Notice the concept called inadequate or overly adequate. Notice the **VOID** universe that it is floating in and allow the label to dissolve. Notice the **NAMELESS ABSOLUTE** underneath it.

Notice the concept called existence or non-existence. Notice that concept and the **VOID** universe in which that concept is floating,. Allow the label called **VOID** universe to dissolve and notice the **NAMELESS ABSOLUTE** underneath it. Notice the concept called alone or connected or fear. Notice the **VOID** it is floating in. Allow the label called **VOID** and notice the **NAMELESS ABSOLUTE** underneath it. Notice the **VOID** universe that contains the concept of incomplete or complete. Allow the label called **VOID** universe to dissolve and notice the **NAMELESS ABSO-LUTE** underneath it. Notice the **VOID** universe which contains the concept of powerless or overly powerful. Allow the label called **VOID** universe to dissolve and notice the **NAMELESS ABSO-LUTE** underneath it.

Notice the **VOID** universe that contains the concept of loveless or love. Allow the label called **VOID** universe to dissolve and notice the **NAMELESS ABSOLUTE** underneath it. Notice the **VOID** universe which contains the concept of control, no control or out of control. Allow the label called **VOID** universe to dissolve and notice the **NAMELESS ABSOLUTE** underneath it. Notice a **VOID** universe where the concept of no safety or safety resides. Allow the label to dissolve and notice the **NAMELESS ABSOLUTE** underneath it. Notice the **VOID** universe where the concept of "I am crazy" or "I have to be sane," healthy or clear. Allow the label and the **VOID** universe to dissolve and be the **NAMELESS ABSOLUTE**. Notice the **VOID** universe that contains the concept of a noticer or an observer or a delabeler. Just allow that **VOID** universe to evaporate.

In a moment, I will ask you to open your eyes and come back into the room.

When the **I AM** arises its universe arises. It is a mere bubble in which the **I AM—VOID** universe resides. You are neither the **I AM** or the bubble universe. You are **BEYOND**.

PARALLEL UNIVERSES

Each **VOID** universe contained within the **NAMELESS AB-SOLUTE** is a parallel universe (**VOID**).

The **NAMELESS ABSOLUTE** is beyond the **VOID** universe which contains the concepts of Superstrings and energy

The **NAMELESS ABSOLUTE** is beyond the **VOID** universes; which ultimately unify through and beyond the **NAME-LESS ABSOLUTE**.

For descriptive terms only, this is the difference between self-realization and God-realization. The realization of **NOT-I-I** is Self Realization. God realization is Beyond Self Realization and even the **VOID OF UNDIFFERENTIATED CONSCIOUS-NESS**. It is the **NAMELESS ABSOLUTE** and it is the **NAME-LESS ABSOLUTE** which erases all other dimensions including the **VOID**, and itself.

In the **NAMELESS ABSOLUTE**, even the **VOID** is gone beyond. Below demonstrates an attempt at this conceptual deconstruction:

CONCLUSION
(IF YOU COULD CALL IT THAT)

When the **VOID** disappears, you enter into **PARABRAMHA** or the **GOD-HEAD**.

The **VOID** universe is a concept within the **NAMELESS ABSOLUTE**. The **VOID** holds the same survival mechanisms as any of its condensations. The **VOID** universes do not know they are **VOID** universes (or even **UNDIFFERENTIATED CON-SCIOUSNESS**), they are not aware of themselves because if they were, they too would disappear and only the **NAMELESS ABSO-LUTE** would remain.

The **VOID** of the **VOID** of Samadhi is when the **VOID** disappears within itself (i.e., reverses the process), and no longer knows itself—in other words, the **VOID VOID**s itself. When this occurs, the **VOID** ends. It is like being in the ocean and finally reaching the shore; the **VOID** dissolves and the **NAMELESS ABSOLUTE** reveals itself.

When you reach the end of the **VOID**, you enter the **PARABRAMHA**, the **GOD-HEAD** or **NAMELESS ABSO-LUTE**. Then the **VOID**(s) disappear(s). Do not settle for the **VOID**. The **NAMELESS** is just beyond.

You can develop multi-dimensional awareness but that goes only to the **NOT-I-I**. It does not include the **VOID**. In the **VOID**, awareness is dissolved. Multi-dimensional awareness and Quantum Psychology disappear in the **VOID** and **BEYOND**. Since the purpose of Quantum Psychology is to find out **WHO YOU ARE**, at this point multi-dimensional awareness and Quantum Psychology with all of its myriad interesting ideas naturally **VOID**s itself. Finally, even the **NAMELESS ABSOLUTE** is no more.

18 •••

EPILOGUE

GOING BEYOND AND WAKING-UP

What Exactly Does "Going Beyond" Mean?

To go beyond means waking-up and questioning every state of consciousness, every Identity, every belief, continually keeping, the awareness that this is not me, but ultimately as **ONE SUBSTANCE** this is me.

Going beyond means moving through and letting go of any attachment or fusion with states, awareness or experiences.

What needs to be understood is that this alleged me or any Ah, this is it! IS NOT IT.

I was once with Maharaj, and a very famous Vipassana (insight meditation) teacher came in and told him about the spiritual practice he was doing, how he had spent many years in Asia studying and teaching this system. Maharaj said to him, "That's not it." The Vipassana teacher looked distraught so the translator leaned over and said, "Don't worry; no matter what you say you are doing, Maharaj always says 'That's not it.'" Let go of systems and techniques. And don't think that Quantum Psychology is it. It is not IT, but rather an Archetype of the Eternal Dismantler looking for something to dismantle. Go Beyond it.

Once one is firmly established in this awareness, then and only then will they be able to let go of even going beyond. On the other hand, I wouldn't give up techniques too early since it has been said, "Don't give up your boat on the ocean of existence until you know how to swim." This was the purpose of the development of multi -dimensional awareness.

This understanding can be important at the start of the illusion of a journey. Most schools, religions, traditions, psychologies and spiritual practices can at best only lead a seeker to the door. Unfortunately for most seekers, however, they are all too often left with a new set of concepts, a new set of identities, and a new set of spiritual rules and regulations which only re-enforce their structures

I have often heard spiritual seekers worrying if they are doing it right and wondering why they aren't experiencing enlightenment. They follow a path cluttered with rules, regulations and cultural baggage and they're in constant fear of making a mistake, losing their direction and blowing it in some way. Many seekers always seem to be waiting for the divine meat ax to fall for their terrible thoughts, irrational feelings and, worse yet, because they yielded to desires. Often a seeker will claim I'm here at last, only to be plummeted into more mental anguish because they did not question the "who" or "I" who was having the "I'm here at last experience."

To let go and go beyond means to go beyond whatever you're told, finally realizing, that it too is a belief, an idea, a concept, a model of truth—but not Truth. One need only question the basic premise which holds the model together, seeing it for what it is, namely, just a concept.

If ever there was an instruction of the simplest and purest principle it is that the "I" who is seeking is the "I" that must be let go of. The "I" that is experiencing is precisely the "I" that must be gone Beyond. The "I" that goes up or down, high or low, must be gone beyond. The "I" that seeks bliss, love or enlightenment must be gone beyond. "You" need to realize that you are beyond anything you think yourself to be, or as Nisargadatta Maharaj, when asked, Who are you? he replied, "Nothing perceivable or conceivable."

What is left, then, is the **SUPREME WITNESS**, beyond the stateless state, a beingless-being, beyond qualities, attributes, **UNDIFFERENTIATED CONSCIOUSNESS** or identities. Beyond even **ESSENCE** or awareness. A student once brought a present to Nisargadatta Maharaj. When he didn't open it, the student asked why and Maharaj said, "I know why you brought the gift—I even know what the gift is. I don't need anything, I don't even need my own self; but I still do arati (worship to my Guru) every day—this is a great mystery."

QUANTUM PSYCHOLOGY PRINCIPLE:

Not until No-I thoughts are identified with will the Great Abyss of the **VOID** become stabilized and available. And then: No You. No Abyss. No **VOID**.

BEYOND is neither **BEYOND** nor not **BEYOND** time, energy, awareness, mass, Witnessing, **I AM**ness, or Space.

It is even beyond the Beingless Being, the Stateless State, yes keep going.

This book is a personal journey that became impersonal. It is the story of a "me" who disappeared in the **VOID** universe and then reappeared in the **VOID** universe only to disappear and reappear. This is the true meaning of reincarnation; it is not physical death and rebirth. Rather the illusion of reincarnation, birth and death is an ongoing natural and spontaneous process which occurs within a **VOID** universe, where the "I" *appears* to be born and then appears to die, at which juncture a new "I" *appears* to be born just a moment later.

When you go beyond the *appearance* of the birth and death of the "I" and stabilize in the **VOID**, recognizing yourself as **THAT ONE SUBSTANCE**, then you might truly go beyond. Then, the great **VOID**, too, will be gone beyond.

A student once said to a Zen master, "My friend is always in the **EMPTINESS**, what should I tell him?" The Zen master said, "Tell him to give up the **EMPTINESS**."

WAKING UP

To bring this to a close seems odd and yet somehow appropriate. Like waking-up from a dream of who "I" thought "I" was and one day realized "I" was NOT.

Nisargadatta Maharaj used to say, "The Guru enters into your dream to tell you it is a dream. They tell you about Enlightenment and try to awaken you from the dream of who you think you are."

Once this occurs—call it Grace, or initiation—the process cannot be stopped. Spiritual practice can and should be only about this, getting that "you" are not the "you" "you" think "you" are, along with the accompanying phenomena both psychological and spiritual which is being used to wake from the dream of **I AM**. Even the techniques and practices and enlightenment occur within the **I AM** bubble dream universe.

Without the understanding that *"you are not"* being repeated again and again, spiritual or psychological practices can only beget more spiritual and psychological practices.

Then, the practitioner starts believing in the dream of psychological and spiritual practice and that there is an "I" doing it—or there is an "I" which will get enlightened).

Upon the realization that, Oh, I thought "I" was (<u>fill in the blank</u>), how strange, **I AM NOT**, does the dream and phenomena end.

For this reason even the quest to answer the question WHO AM I disappears because it suggests that there is a you who *is* something.

In Zen Buddhism it is said that Enlightenment is like waking from a dream where both the person in the dream and the dream itself (i.e., dream visions) disappear.

So too, **ESSENCE, VOID** and the **NAMELESS ABSOLUTE** disappear as the dream and the dreamer disappear. Because they are all MIND and PART of the dream.

This is why Ramana Maharishi said that a dream and the waking state are the same because they both occur to the dreamer within the dream only. Like a mirage of water appearing in the desert which disappears as you move toward it, so too everything disappears upon waking-up.

Wake-up to the dream and realize that all you see, know, hear, understand and experience, including **VOID, GOD, NAMELESS,** etc., can only be there as long as you are asleep imagining *you are* or **I AM—AWAKE**. When you wake-up *you* and all this too and everything will disappear as if by magic.

Even the idea of dreaming and waking-up to **I AM NOT** are also part of the dream-mirage.

Good-bye for now,
With Love
Your Brother
Stephen

19 ●●●

BEYOND

THERE IS NO BEYOND!

REFERENCES •••

Agneesens, C. *Fabric of Wholeness: Biological Intelligence and Relational Gravity*. (Quantum Institute, CA, 2000)

Almaas, A. H. (1986). *The void*. York Beach: Samuel Weiner, Inc.

American College Dictionary. (1963). New York: Random House.

Arica Institute, Inc., The. (1989). The Arican. New York.

Bahirjit, B. B. (1963). *The Amritanubhava of Janadeva*. Bombay: Sirun Press.

Bentov, I. (1977). *Stalking the wild pendulum*. Rochester VT: Destiny Books.

Blanck, G., & Rubin. *Ego psychology II*. New York: Columbia Univ. Press.

Blanck, G., & Rubin. (1979). *Ego psychology II: Psychoanalytic developmental psychology*. New York: Columbia University Press.

Bohm, D. (1951). *Quantum theory*. London: Constable.

Bohm, D. (1980). *Wholeness and the implicate order*. London: Ark Paperbacks.

Bohm, D. (1985). *Unfolding meaning.* London: Ark Paperbacks.

Bohm, D., & Peat, D. F. (1987)). *Science, Order and Creativity.* New York: Bantam Books.

Bollas, C. (1987). *The shadow of the object: Psychoanalysis of the unthought known.* New York: Columbia Univ. Press

Bollas, C. (1989). *Furies of destine: Psychoanalysis and human idiom.* London: Free Association Volumes

Bourland, D., & Johnson, P. (1991). *To Be or Not: An e-prime anthology.* San Francisco: International Society for General Semantics.

Buddhist Text Translation Society. (1980*). The heart sutra and commentary.* San Francisco: Buddhist Text Translation Society.

Capra, F. (1976). *The tao of physics.* New York: Bantam Books.

Edinger, E. (n.d.). *Ego and the archetype: Individualization and the religious function of the archetype.* Publisher unknown

Gleick, James. (1987). *Chaos.* New York: Penguin Volumes.

Godman, D. (1985). *The teachings of Ramana Maharishi.* Ankara, London.

Hawkins, S. (1988). *A brief history of time.* New York: Bantam Volumes.

Herbert, N. (1985). *Quantum reality.* New York: Anchor Press.

Horner, A. J. (1985). *Object relations and the developing ego in therapy.* Northridge, NJ: Jason Arunsun, Inc.

Hua, Master Tripitaka. (1980). *Shurangama sutra.* San Francisco: Buddhist Text Translation Society

Ichazo, O. (1993). *The fourteen pillars of perfect recognition.* New York: The Arica Institute, Inc.

Isherwood, C., & Prahnavarla, Swami. (1953). *How to know God: The yoga of Patanjali.* CA: New American Library.

Johnson, S. M. (1987). *Humanizing the narcissistic style.* New York: The Arica Institute, Inc.

Johnson, S. M. (1991). *The symbiotic character.* NY/London: W. W. Norton & Co.

Kaku, M. (1994). *Hyperspace.* New York: Anchor-Doubleday Volumes.

Kaku M. (1987). *Beyond Einstein: The cosmic quest for the theory of the universe.* New York: Bantam Volumes.

Korzybski, A. (1993). *Science and sanity.* Englewood, NJ: Institute for General Semantics.

Korzybski, A. (1962). *Selections from science and sanity.* Englewood, NJ: International Non-Aristotelian Library Publishing Company.

Irving J. L. (1941). *Language habits in human affairs.* England, New Jersey: International Society for General Semantics

Mahler, M. (1968). *On the human symbiosis and vicissitudes of individuation.* New York: International Universe Press.

Marshall, R. J., & Marshall, S. V. (1988). *The transference-countertransference matrix: The emotional-cognitive dialogue in psychotherapy, psychoanalysis and supervision.* New York: Columbia University Press.

Mckay, M., D., M., & Fanning, P. (1981). *Thoughts and feelings: The art of cognitive stress intervention.* Oakland, CA: Harbinger Publications.

Miller, H. (1961). *Tropic of cancer*. New York: Grove Press.

Miller, H. (1961). *Tropic of capricorn*. New York: Grove Press.

Muktananda, Swami. (1974). *Play of consciousness*. Ganeshpuri: Shree Gurudev Ashram.

Muktananda, Swami. (1978). *I am that: The science of hamsa*. New York: S.Y.D.A. Foundation.

Mookerjit, Ajit. (1971). *Tantra asana. A way to self-realization*. Basel, Paris, New Delhi: Ravi Kumar.

Naranjo, C. (1990). *Enneatype structures: Self analysis for the seeker*. CA: Gateways IDHHB, Inc.

Nicoll, M. (1984*). Psychological commentaries on the teaching of Gurdjieff and Ouspensky*. Vol. 1. Boulder/London: Shambhala.

Nisargadatta, Maharaj. *I am That*. 1994. Durham, NC: Acorn Press

Ouspensky, P. D. *In search of the miraculous*. 1949. New York: Harcourt, Brace and World, Inc.

Palmer, H. (1988). *The enneagram*. CA: Harper & Row.

Peat, D. F. (1987). *The bridge between matter and mind*. New York: Bantam Books.

Peat, D. F. (1988). *Superstrings and the search for the theory of everything*. Chicago: Contemporary Volumes.

Peat, D. F., & Briggs, J. (1989). *The turbulent mirror: An illustrated guide to chaos theory & the science of wholeness*. New York: Harper & Row, 1989.

Peat, D. F. (1990). *Einstein's moon: Bell's theorem and the curious quest for quantum reality*. Chicago: Contemporary Books.

Peat, D. F. (1991). *The philosopher's stone: Chaos, synchronicity, and the hidden order of the world.* New York: Bantam Books.

Reich, W. (1942). *The function of the orgasm.* The discovery of the orgone. New York: World Publishing.

Riso, D. R. (1987). *Personality types: Using the enneagram for self-discovery.* Boston: Houghton Mifflin Company.

Riso, D. R. (1988). *Understanding the enneagram.* Massachusetts: Houghton Mifflin Company.

Riso, D. R. (1987). *Humanizing the narcissistic style.* NY/London: W.W. Norton & Co.

Shah, I. (1978). *Learning how to learn: Psychology and spirituality in the Sufi Way.* London: Octagon Press

Shah, I. (1978). *A perfumed scorpion: The way to the way.* San Francisco: Harper & Row

Shakaran, R. (1991). *The spirit of homeopathy.* Bombay: Homeopathic Medical Publishers.

Singh, J. (1963). *Pratyabhijnahrdeyam: The secret of self recognition.* Delhi: Motilal Banarsidass.

Singh, J. (1979). *Siva Sutra, the yoga of Supreme Identity.* Delhi: Motilal Banarsidass.

Singh, J. (1979). *Vijnanabhairava or divine consciousness.* Delhi: Motilal Banarsidass.

Singh, J. (1980). *Spanda Karikas.* Delhi: Motilal Banarsidass.

Suzuki, S. *Zen mind, beginner's mind.* New York: Weatherhill, 1970.

Talbot, M. (1981). *Mysticism and the new physics.* New York: Bantam Books.

Talbot, M. (1987). *Beyond the quantum*. New York: Bantam Books.

Talbot, M. (1991). *The holographic universe*. New York: Harper Collins.

Vithoukas, G. (1980). *The science of homeopathy*. New York: Grove Press.

Weinberg, H. L. (1959*). Levels of knowing and existence: Studies in general semantics*. Englewood, NJ: Institute of General Semantics.

Wolinsky, S. H. (1993). *The dark side of the inner child*. Norfolk, CT: Bramble Co.

Wolinsky, S. H. (1991). *Trances people live: Healing approaches to quantum psychology*. Norfolk, CT: Bramble Co.

Wolinsky, S. H. (1993). *Quantum consciousness*. Norfolk, CT: Bramble Books.

Wolinsky, S. H. (1995). *Hearts on Fire*. Norfolk, CT: Bramble Books.

Wolinsky, S. H. (1994). *The tao of chaos: Quantum consciousness*. Vol. II. Norfolk, CT: Bramble Books.

Wolinsky, S. H. (1999). *The way of the human*. Vol. 1: *Developing multi-dimensional awareness*. CA: Quantum Institute Press.

Wolinsky, S. H. (1999). *The way of the human*. Vol. II: *The False Core-False Self*. CA: Quantum Institute Press.

Wolinsky, S. H. (1999). *The way of the human*. Vol. III: *Beyond Quantum Psychology*. CA: Quantum Institute Press.

Wolinsky, S. H. (2000). *I AM THAT I AM: A tribute to Sri Nisargadatta Maharaj*. CA: Quantum Institute Press.

Wolinsky, S. H. (2000). *Intimate relationship: Why they do and do not work*. CA: Quantum Institute Press.